WRITERS REPUBLIC

THE MANIFESTO

OF AN ABORIGINAL DESCENDANT

OF NORTH AMERICAN INDIGENOUS PEOPLE

JESUS ANGEL CARRERA

WRITERS REPUBLIC L.L.C.
515 Summit Ave. Unit R1
Union City, NJ 07087, USA

Website: *www.writersrepublic.com*
Hotline: *1-877-656-6838*
Email: *info@writersrepublic.com*

Ordering Information:
Quantity sales. Special discounts are available on quantity purchases by corporations, associations, and others. For details, contact the publisher at the address above.

Library of Congress Control Number:		2020932943
ISBN-13:	978-1-64620-238-6	[Paperback Edition]
	978-1-64620-486-1	[Hardback Edition]
	978-1-64620-239-3	[Digital Edition]

Rev. date: 02/20/2025

CONTENTS

Poesía

PATRIA

A CHANT FROM THE POOR

My life is one of the things I love the most
My appreciation to such thing gives me hope
Blessed are the peacemakers who stand against corruption
Blessed are the ones who improve humanity and blossom

Only the poor understand such need
Only the humble man will listen to this plea
How sad it is to see great men get powerful then fall
How sad it is to see children hungry and cold

Poetry had made up this song
Reality is written in these words
Come and listen to the poor
Come to set us free like the morning dawn

A flower will grow if it's watered or moist
A hummingbird will get close if the flower is nurtured with love
How sweet is the honey, I'll tell you, bro
How pleasant is its flavor
Come and join me so

This festival will bind you together with the poor
This fellowship will give us life, bro, forever and forevermore

ABORIGINAL DESCENDANTS OF THE AMERICAS

My beautiful people
With their beautiful mind
My wonderful people
Who found many ways to survive

Decolonization is attached in our hearts
Emancipation is searched in our everyday lives
Five hundred years of suppression
Five hundred years of assimilation

Resisting globalization
Ending alienation
First civilization
Surviving extermination
It is our everyday job

War against us
It needs to be stopped

Aboriginal descendants of the Americas,
We need to wake up
Study the past
Give each other a hand

It is for our survival in our own land
Love each other with dignity and pride
Don't push yourselves down like done in the past
Analyze our own obstacles in life

Come up with solutions to overcome and survive
Survival of the oldest tribes
It is the new generation's objective and job

Long live our dignity and pride
Long live our new generation anywhere we stand

Blending cultures in the melting pot
This new generation will never be stopped
Biracial and multiracial is in our blood
Indigenous roots makes us natives to this land

Aboriginal descendants of the Americas,
We need to wake up
Study the past
Give each other a hand

It is for our survival in our own land
Love each other with dignity and pride
Don't push yourselves down like done in the past
Analyze our own obstacles in life

Come up with solutions to overcome and survive
Survival of the oldest tribes
It is the new generation's objective and job

Long live our dignity and pride
Long live our new generation anywhere we stand

Blending cultures in the melting pot
This new generation will never be stopped
Biracial and multiracial is in our blood
Indigenous roots makes us natives to this land

ACCEPTANCE

I am a simple man, brothers and sisters
I am a poet
I am a peacemaker, brothers and sisters
I am life's lover

I am humanity in times of persecution
I am my brother's keeper in times of disillusion
I am the voice of the voiceless
I am a humble man

I am the survivor
I am the oppressed
I am the future generation, brothers and sisters
I am the new mixture of one human race

I do not like dividing myself
I do not like suppressing myself
I'd rather be loved, brothers and sisters
And be accepted by my fellow men

DANCING THROUGH LIFE

Dancing with the moon!
Traveling through space!
Feeling a good mood!
Casting everything away!

I know many people are gone!
I know I'm still living on!
I know many people are sad!
I know I'm still living my life!

No bitterness will keep me down!
No politics will tie me down!
I will fear no torment!
I will fear no lament!

'Cause I'm dancing with the moon!
'Cause I'm traveling through space!
'Cause I'm feeling a good mood!
'Cause I'm casting everything away!

Do not use politics to keep me down!
Do not use philosophies to make me smile!
Do not use your system and your bureaucracy!
Do not use your money and your hypocrisy!

'Cause I'm dancing with the moon!
'Cause I'm traveling through space!
'Cause I'm feeling a good mood!
'Cause I'm casting everything away!

How sweet it is to dance!
How sweet is the sound!
Once I was lost
(Once I was lost, babe)
Once I was lost,
But now I am found!

No bitterness will keep me down!
No politics will tie me down!
I will fear no torment!
I will fear no lament!

'Cause I'm dancing with the moon!
'Cause I'm traveling through space!
'Cause I'm feeling a good mood!
'Cause I'm casting everything away!

Do not use politics to keep me down!
Do not use philosophies to make me smile!
Do not use your system and your bureaucracy!
Do not use your money and your hypocrisy!

'Cause I'm dancing with the moon!
'Cause I'm traveling through space!
'Cause I'm feeling a good mood!
'Cause I'm casting everything away!

How sweet is to dance!
How sweet is the sound!
Once I was lost
(Once I was lost, babe)
Once I was lost,
But now I am found!

ALIENS IN OUR OWN LAND

I got culture and deep roots!
My ancestors were good people too!
All the negative views were written for genocidal use!
I'm no longer confused!

I can see the truth!
I am able to notice the conqueror's intentions too!
Our history was twisted in their old books!
Mesoamerica was divided into many countries too!

Native people lost everything (now we're on the loot)!
Looking for a brighter future, boo!
We are in the loop, so please don't shoot!
Now you see me explaining this realistic truth!

Observe very carefully the way this system rules!
Look how many people are dying everywhere too!

I see you, and I see my own life!
I think critically about my people's present and past!
I try not to be bias and divide us on these lines!
I try to consciously speak up my own mind!

I create new rhymes coming from my heart!
I try to find understanding on this sweet life!
I do wipe the tears on my eyes from time to time!
I still got too much love to provide!

We need to understand our own future and past!
We need to find new ways to survive!
Borders divided our old tribes!
We no longer recognize who we truly are!

Confusion among many of us!
Extermination upon my own kind!
Alienation among the ones who survived!
Segregation and isolation is stopping us!

This new political-economical system enslaved us for life!
We became aliens in our own land!
There is partiality and no equality for many of us!

Native men, we need to survive!
Human race, we need to unite!
We need to find a new way of life!
We need to bring acceptance and true love for all mankind!

ALL I NEED IS MY MUSIC

I don't need any chemicals to get me high, brother!
I don't need any chemicals to get me high, sister!
All I need is my music, brother!
All I need is my music, sister

All I need is my music
To fulfill this thirst from my heart!
I dance to my music because I am alive!
I dance to my music because it heals the pain deep inside!

Look at the trees!
Look at the grass!
Look at the ocean!
Look at the sky!
Look at the moon shining so bright!

No bitterness will get me down!
No loneliness will overthrow my beautiful smile!
Heaven would be on earth, brothers!
Heaven would be on earth, sisters!

If it wasn't for people that are keeping everything to themselves!
Heaven would be on earth, brothers!
Heaven would be on earth, sisters!
If it wasn't for people that are corrupting everything on their way!

O hear this spiritual cry, Lord!
O hear this pain from our soul!
Hear this lamentation, Lord!
Hear this torment and sorrow coming from the poor!

We are forced to believe that everything is in peace!
But this peace brings no peace in real life!
We need true love and justice for all mankind!
We need redemption with true affection in our hearts!

Because everyone talks about justice all the time!
But this justice brings no justice when their ego is in their hearts!

And I don't need any chemicals to get me high, brother!
I don't need any chemicals to get me high, sister!
All I need is my music, brother!
All I need is my music, sister

All I need is my music
To fulfill this thirst from my heart!
I dance to my music because I am alive!
I dance to my music because it heals the pain deep inside!

Look at the trees!
Look at the grass!
Look at the ocean!
Look at the sky!
Look at the moon shining so bright!

No bitterness will get me down!
No loneliness will overthrow my beautiful smile!
Heaven would be on earth, brothers!
Heaven would be on earth, sisters!

If it wasn't for people that are keeping everything to themselves!
Heaven would be on earth, brothers!
Heaven would be on earth, sisters!
If it wasn't for people that are corrupting everything in their way!

CHRISTOPHER COLUMBUS

Columbus, slave master,
The Indian has come!
He has brought you gold and silver
On the day you arrived!

Please don't rape my sisters and kill the little ones!
Please don't spread any disease among any of us!
Let me live my life in peace with my corn plants!
Let me live emancipated from the other empires in my native land!

Your arrival conquered and slaughtered many of us!
In the war for the Americas, I managed to survive!
You destroyed my cities, temples, and gave me a Christian name!
In the name of the Almighty, I now cry many tears just in vain!

You stole my history and placed me as your own personal slave!
You brought to us a new system just to enrich yourself!
You forced us to speak only the European languages!
You categorized Indians as inferior people and savages!

I now continue fighting against prejudiced people everywhere I go!
I still work hard, labor, and heal my psychological wounds with
marijuana and alcohol!
I was born a mestizo, and I am the new generation!
I try to look for ways to stop passing on this old transgression!

I did survive and blended in!
Not just in my skin but in this whole society!
I do defeat supremacy with my own beliefs!
I do want full equality and start my own family!

I do want my kids to be all what they can be!
I do want them to see their dreams come through as it should be!
I don't want their generation to stop reaching their full potential!
I do want my children to reach a higher education!

I'm still claiming for full equality for all mankind!
I'm still fighting with rhymes and knowledge stuck in my mind!

Columbus Day should be eliminated!
Indigenous People's Days (not just one day) should be appreciated!

DECOLONIZE YOUR MIND

Open up your heart
Decolonize your mind
Free up your spirit
Understand your past

Live up your present
Focus on your future
Be cautious and strategize
Look for new ways to survive

History books are full of lies
They explain to you one perspective
Forgetting the oppressed ones
Money and power is in their mind

Human understanding is on these lines
Survival of the indigenous tribes
Borders separated us
It alienated us
And exterminated many of us

We need to unite
We need to survive
We are not aliens
We are in our own land

Let's make a pact
Let's give us a hand
Let's move forward
Let's speak up

A bullet can shut us up
But this understanding will forever survive

We are revolutionaries
We cannot be contrary
We are all visionaries
We have to protect ourselves from mercenaries

Survival is in our plan
We cannot just give up
Come let us unite
For a brighter future to come

I'm speaking out my truth
I'm speaking out for you
I'm backing you up
I hope you do the same too

We cannot be confused
It's understandable, boo
Don't be alarmed
We are calling for you

Study your past
Understand your present
Focus on the future
Be cautious and strategize

Open up your heart
Decolonize your mind
Be supersmart
Look for new ways to survive
Be cautious and strategize

Survival of the indigenous tribes
Borders separated us
It alienated us
And exterminated many of us

We need to unite
We need to survive
We are not aliens
We are in our own land

DANCING AND SINGING

It is a beautiful and bright day today, my dear friends
It is a pleasant, relaxing, and chilled day

The sound of the waves are stuck in my head
The palm trees are singing along with the flying birds
The dancing of the ocean is making my heart so content
The smell of the flowers is helping to release myself

I'm dancing with the ocean waves
I'm singing with the flying birds
I'm so content
I'm so amazed

I'm dancing, baby
I'm singing, darling
I'm so relieving myself
I'm dancing with the ocean waves

I'm singing with the flying birds
I'm so content
I'm so amazed
I'm so happy to be here in this lovely day

The night is falling,
But it's okay
It will be so great to appreciate
The beautiful sunset

I'm dancing with the ocean waves
I'm singing with the flying birds
I'm so content
I'm so amazed

I'm so happy to be here in this lovely day
The high tides are carrying my problems away
The flying birds are singing with me today
The dancing waves are lifting my head in this getaway

The sunset is so beautiful to appreciate
And I'm dancing with the ocean waves
And I'm singing with the flying birds
I'm so content

I'm so amazed to be here in this lovely day
I'm so happy and so blessed
I'm so thankful to Mother Earth
It has me dancing with the moving waves

It has me singing with the flying birds

I'm so content, my dear friends
I'm so amazed to be enjoying this beautiful day
It has me dancing with the moving waves
It has me singing with the flying birds

I'm not stressed
I'm not upset
I'm so content
I'm so amazed

To be dancing with the moving waves
And to be singing with the flying birds

EMANCIPATING MYSELF

I'm the master of my own destiny
I'm the ruler of everything within me

The flesh you see
The words I speak
The strength on my feet
The air I breathe

My life is everything to me
No material things can change me within
No hypocrisy can corrupt my destiny

Because I am humanity in times of brutality
Because I am solidarity in times of a big tragedy

My mentality is love and not hate
Unification is the key rather than seeking for revenge
Love your neighbors in times of distress
Hate racism every single moment that you can

No modern slavery can defeat me today
No xenophobia can segregate me tonight
The hours passed,
And in my heart, there's only love kept inside

I'm enslaving myself for this new system
I have assimilated myself to survive
I am alienated by the conquerors and slave masters in my own
land

I'm no illegal alien, as portrayed in the media
I'm an aboriginal descendant living in the Americas for a very long
time
Long history has never been told in real life
Long existence in the whole continent who truly survived

Mestizo with love and pride
Emancipating myself through these rhymes
Flowing like the wind in the deep blue sky
Telling the truth as it has never been told
Sending love to my people, maintaining self-control

And here I go in this hateful world educating myself and moving
on
I keep my peace in my soul as I carry on
I tell this true for my people born out of true love

EXPOSING THESE TRUTHS

My heart is beating in harmony!
My mind is resting in peace!
My love is for all humanity!
My strength comes from within!

I see my own struggles
I seek for solutions in me!
I come to you and smile!
I rest and keep my peace!

I know what I am!
I know where I'm from!
I know where I'm going to!
I know how to keep my strength!

My roots were destroyed by the conquerors!
My land was kept among them!
My history was twisted to dehumanize me!
My riches were stolen by them

This political-economical system enslaved us!
This lack of understanding imprisoned me!
These borders alienated us!
This understanding is setting me free!

I got soul and deep roots!
I got pride and love shining for you
I got redemption and truth!
I got unification through exposing these truths!

My heart, babe, is beating in harmony!
My mind, darling, is resting in peace!
My love is for all humanity, boo!
My strength comes from within!

FEEL THE LOVE

Let's recognize the manifold stupidities of mankind!
Let's bring satisfaction and affection closer to people's hearts!

What belongs to Mother Nature belongs to Mother Nature itself!
What belongs to men belongs to every single man!

There is no reason to take away anybody's bread!
There is no need to enslave another fellow man!

Please do not treat me wrong for the color of my skin!
Please do not mistreat me for my cultural being!

You have to eliminate the whole philosophy of supremacy on me!
You have to be humble and start looking for acceptance!

Because the Creator provides this true freedom upon ourselves!
Because the Designer created us in his image to be fruitful on
Mother Earth!

So we have to free ourselves from these wasteful mentality and
medieval ways!
We have to set ourselves free and start giving people a chance!

Nationalities will no longer have significance!
The ideal society will no longer have any indifferences!

Because there will be only one human race!
Because love will rule the world, and everyone will be treated the same!

We have to find new strategies for unification!
We have to come together as one people and one nation!

We have to reach out to the marginalized communities!
We have to work it out and assimilate positive strategies!

We have to accept ourselves, love ourselves, and make it work!
We have to eliminate any resentment and replace it with true love!

So we can finally flourish and prosper in this society!
So we can all feel the love and live the results of this full equality!

FELLOWSHIP

Water is the element of life
Water quenches the thirst of my heart
Earth is the place we stand
Earth brings about reproduction and new life

Fire brings about purification
Fire protects my body from any infection
Wind composes the air we breathe
Wind will lead my soul to the east

Harmony brings about peace
Tranquility brings about freedom within
Acceptance is the answer here
Humanity is definitely in me

Fellowship is what we all need
Prosperity is what your brethren is asking thee
Listen to what he says
Listen to this one claim

Listen to the oppressed
Listen to the poor request
So we can finally be friends
And bring about prosperity across the earth

"FLOWETRY" FROM THE SOUL

Man, you know it's hard to live a straight life!
Among people who don't know who you really are!

It's hard enough to find our own path toward the light!
It's hard enough to see a brighter future ahead of us!
It is painful enough to describe our sinful life!
Without hope and love throughout the stages of time!

Because I don't want to give up my hope!
But keep on dreaming in a real dream!
Until this same dream becomes real to me!

Because life goes on,
And I'm still trapped in the same zone
Of poverty, rejections, and hateful political laws!

I speak up out of love
(I resist and survive in this cruel world!)
I tell the truth as it goes
(I am the survivor of this genocidal war!)

I describe beauty without flaws
(My native people must survive on this future to come!)
I face hateful laws
(Colonization since five hundred years ago!)

I comprehend and move on
(Unification must be met to lift up the poor!)
I definitely got soul
(Blood of the oppressed people is in my bones!)

I got heart
(I love my own people plenty enough!)
I manage to keep control
(I rise in this new movement among some of us!)

I feel love
(My soul is brighter when hard times come!)
Here comes my flow
(Performing creativity with peaceful psalms!)

Come on

Amando a mi gente de corazón, sangre y pulmón!
Con mucha razón y sentimiento de un verdadero Amor!
Loca pasión y entendimiento es lo que siento hoy! Salvaje?
No! Eso no soy!
Que maldicion es amar sin ser amado con la misma intención!

This is my flow enlightening my soul
Using creativity to empower the poor
Keeping control
Passing a joint
Releasing good vibes and moving on

FLY AWAY, LITTLE BIRD

The eagle loves the mountains!
The dolphin loves the seas!
To each its own desires!
To each and one of them free!

No man could understand how lovely this life is!
No man could understand how each person is created within!

There is confusion in our mind!
There is lots of pain in our heart!
There is jealousy and hatred upon mankind!
While the beautiful sun is embracing the seven seas with the
sunlight!

We might not have the power to change all things!
We might not have the power to set everyone free!
We might not have the power to stop people's grief!
But we have the same desires to follow the same dream!

Fly, O bird, fly
(Fly, little bird, away!)
Fly, O bird, fly
(Fly, little bird, away!)
Fly, O bird, fly
(Fly, little bird, away!)

Don't let the hunter catch you asleep on your nest!
Don't let corruption destroy you today!

Que bonito, que bonito,
It is to see the flying birds flying, muy despacito!

Don't let anyone confuse you!
Don't let anyone amuse you!
Don't let anyone deceive you!
Don't let anyone think for you!

We don't want to conquer anybody!
We don't want to enslave anybody!
We don't want to follow any selfish desires!
We don't want to exploit anybody!

We just want to live life away from any grief!

Please, I beg you now, do not treat me wrong!
Please, I beg you now, do not mistreat me anymore!

'Cause humanity is me!
'Cause humanity is you!
'Cause humanity is all the children starving for food!

You have to eliminate the whole philosophy of supremacy!
You have to humble yourself and start thinking equally!

'Cause there is no need to take anybody's bread!
'Cause there is no need to enslave a fellow man!
'Cause humanity is me!
'Cause humanity is you!
'Cause humanity is all the children starving for food!

Fly, O bird, fly
(Fly, little bird, away!)
Fly, O bird, fly
(Fly, little bird, away!)
Fly, O bird, fly
(Fly, little bird, away!)

Don't let the hunter catch you asleep on your nest!
Don't let corruption destroy you today!

FLYING AWAY

I will fly and fly away!
I will fly and fly and be at rest!
I will fly in the time machine like a flying bird!
I will fly from iniquity from place to place!
I will fly and look for freedom within!

The sun shines
O dear sister, the flowers bloom!
The day is so bright
O dear brother, don't feel blue!

Don't let the wicked control the thoughts in your head!
Don't let the oppressors make you feel so much less!
'Cause no matter what they do to you or they might say!
You were made like an iron sword with a burning flame!

Don't let anyone put you to shame!
Don't let anyone eliminate your happiness with distress!
Don't let anyone lead you astray!
Don't let anyone take your freedom away!

'Cause no matter what they do to you or they might say!
You were made like an iron sword with a burning flame!
Be glad and don't look back!
And open up your heart!

Bless the ones who persecute you!
For they walk in life with their blind eyes!
Their deeds have become wicked!
Their delights have become corrupted!
With the blood of the little ones!

Remember your first love, dear sister!
Think twice and don't lose control!
Remember the golden city, dear brother!
Remain strong and don't lose hope!

I will fly and fly away!
I will fly and fly and be at rest!
I will fly in the time machine like a flying bird!
I will fly from iniquity from place to place!
I will fly and look for freedom within!

FREE YOURSELVES

Hey, Brother Man
(Brother Man!)
Why do you oppress the oppressed!

Hey, Mr. Minuteman
(Mr. Minuteman!)
Why do you terrorize the oppressed!

Hey, Mr. System Man
(Mr. System Man!)
Why do you force us to compete against ourselves!

Hey, Mr. Merchant Man
(Mr. Merchant Man!)
Why do you raise the prices every single day!

I cry,
O yes, I cry!
I cry for equal opportunities for the oppressed!

'Cause as long as I'm alive!
'Cause as long as I'm alive!
I'm gonna search for freedom along my way!
'Cause my life and my love for true freedom defines myself!

Look at the children standing along the way!
Look at the poor starving every day!
Look at the beautiful people uprising everywhere!

Yeah, free yourselves, little sisters
(Free yourselves!)
Free yourselves, little brothers
(Free yourselves!)

Free yourselves
From this social captivity every day!
Free yourselves
From this poverty everywhere!

Uprise everyone (Unite)
Strike Everywhere (Walkout)
Stand up for justice (Don't give up)
Rise up from injustice (Don't be alarmed)

We are not illegal aliens (together we stand)
We are theoretically speaking in our mother land
I say, We are not illegal aliens (together we stand)
We are theoretically speaking in our mother land

Look at the children standing along the way!
Look at the poor starving every day!
Look at the beautiful people uprising everywhere!

Yeah, free yourselves, little sisters
(Free yourselves!)
Free yourselves, little brothers
(Free yourselves!)

Free yourselves
From this social captivity every day!
Free yourselves
From this poverty everywhere!

Uprise everyone (Unite)
Strike Everywhere (Walkout)
Stand up for justice (Don't give up)
Rise up from injustice (Don't be alarmed)

We are not illegal aliens (together we stand)
We are theoretically speaking in our mother land
I say, We are not illegal aliens (together we stand)
We are theoretically speaking in our mother land

FREEDOM FIGHTER

Freedom fighter, stand up
Freedom fighter, exercise your rights
Freedom fighter, don't give up
Freedom fighter, unite for this cause

Show some respect, brother man
Don't try to intimidate me
Show me some love, little sister
Don't try to segregate me

In this world of competition
Sending love is my mission
Money is just an illusion
Full equality is the solution

We will break stereotypes
We will find freedom in our path
Uprise everywhere
(Unite)
Walkout on the streets
(Strike)

Fight for your freedom today
No man is illegal, we say
This is our motherland
No time to cry and advance

Freedom fighter, stand up
Freedom fighter, exercise your rights
Freedom fighter, don't give up
Freedom fighter, unite for this cause

Legalize humanity
Decolonize this society
Tell the children the truth
Educate our future youth

Let us march in unity
Let us stand up as a community
Let our liberties be used
Let our voices be heard

Love is the key to be unified
Freedom is given to all mankind
Respect for who we are
Uprising is necessary for us to survive

Human rights violations,
This is my people's lamentations
Full equality is the main foundation
We're crying of poverty and starvation

Freedom fighter, stand up
Freedom fighter, exercise your rights
Freedom fighter, don't give up
Freedom fighter, unite for this cause

FREEDOM WITHIN

I could see the sun
Across the golden sky!
I could see the moon
When the day turns into dark!

I could see the ocean, the mountains, and the valleys, babe,
When the rain is gone from my sight!
I could see you better, honey,
When I'm holding you tight!

Tu amor esta lleno de encanto por eso,
Mi nena (por eso) esta canción te canto!
Tus besos son como agua de coco,
Por eso, mi reyna, (por eso) tu me vuelves loco!

Chanting through the valleys and the cities!
Together chanting to unify the poor!
Chanting through the fields and the rallies!
Together chanting for happiness and love!

The children will unite my friends!
The humble man will be upraised!
The peacemakers will resist any tribulation!
In any trouble to keep themselves alive!

Terrorizing the poor brothers
Will not give you any control!
Oppressing the humble men
Will only give you more remorse!
Fighting against your brothers
Will only separate you even more!

The children will unite!
The humble men will be upraised!
The peacemakers will resist temptation
(In any trouble)
To keep themselves alive!

The waters move
Freely across the earth!
The air I breathe
Runs into my veins!

It runs into my lungs,
It runs into my blood!
It runs into my heart,
It runs into my soul!
It brings me freedom again!

Harmony, babe,
Possesses tranquility!
Equality, honey,
Brings us integrity!

Honesty, darling,
Gives us peacefulness!
It gives us love!
It gives us strength and freedom within!

FULL EQUALITY

This love that I feel for you is unconditional!
It's the loving part of me that gets too emotional!
It's the ultimate feeling of true love!
It's the natural emotion coming from my soul!

You gave me shelter when I needed it the most!
You provided all the elements that helped me to grow!
You thought me the main principles of humanity!
You gave me the strength to look for equality!

You encouraged me to think critically!
You showed me to question everything!
You helped me to identify xenophobia in each situation!
The marginalized way for individuals to classify this momentum!

You showed me not to fear the unjust!
You taught me to analyze our own history and past!
History was written by the dominant culture!
Our history and land were taken and devoured by old vultures!

Let's forgive and forget about this fact!
Let's focus in a greater future to come!
Let's leave everything behind!
Let's rebuild a better future for all mankind!

Let us move forward in this society!
Let us grow economically!
Teach us to grow intellectually!
Grant us the privilege to reach full equality!

INNER SELF (CONFESSION)

Love can overcome anything
Hate can only create more iniquity
Respect is an action of humanity
Disrespect is an action of brutality

I am a civilized man
I am educated by a higher man
I am someone who appreciates culture from everywhere
I am an Afro-Mestizo created on earth

I am the music given to men
I am the gift given to Mother Earth
I am a new poet from which I stand
I am an offspring of human race

I am someone who understands the beautiful values of being
human among this human race

FULL EQUALITY FOR THE INDIGENOUS COMMUNITIES

Live and let others live in harmony
Live and give others equal opportunity
Give others the opportunity to succeed
Give others full equality

Equal opportunity is what we all need, baby
The plea from the oppressed is requested here
We don't need partiality in history, honey
Humanity is the reason for this liberty

Dignity is the key to rise in this society, darling
Representing the little kids in cages of the Latin American
community

Live and let others live in harmony, brother
Live and give others equal opportunity
Give others the opportunity to succeed, sister
Give others full equality

Claiming human right violations as we all can see
I call upon liberty and breath
I call upon upon this reality and live
I call upon the lady of justice and see
I call upon our present history and sing

You are the oxygen that my lungs need
You are the food that my spirit seeks
You are the queen of my everyday dreams
You are our liberty

You are our history
You are our equality
You are full of compassion
And human understanding
To you, I confess this poetry

To you, my darling, I claim for peace
Because you are the hope that my soul seeks
Because you are the blood that my eyes see
Because you are the justice that we all need
Because you are the liberty of every human being

You are what my body needs
You are my spiritual relief
You prevent and relieve any conspiracy
You are the reality that the common people live

You are the true evidence of morality
You are the example of what is supposed to be
Live and let others live in harmony, brother
Live and give others equal opportunity

Give others the opportunity to succeed, sister
Give others full equality

GOTTA LET YOU KNOW YOUR FALLACIES

Criollo, I gotta love you!
Criollo, you gotta educate yourself!

Your people came from Europe and stayed!
Your people came and enslaved my indigenous people on the way!
You call me an alien, but you don't see yourself!
Your people came from the Old World, keep it in your head

You were born in this place, you say
And yet you claim to be a native as I am!

You are a hypocrite to yourself!
You don't love me!
You want to keep me uneducated and distressed!

We follow your dirty game!
We enslave ourselves for your system
You terrorize us with your laws so we can obey

We work and work for the minimum wage
We work and work to the maximum stage
We work and work so you can enrich yourself

Criollo, I gotta love you!
Criollo, you gotta educate yourself!

Your people came from Europe and stayed!
Your people came and enslaved my indigenous people on the way!
You call me an alien, but you don't see yourself!
Your people came from the Old World, keep it in your head

You were born in this place, you say
And yet you claim to be a native as I am!

You are a hypocrite to yourself!
You don't love me!
You want to keep me uneducated and distressed!

We follow your dirty game!
We enslave ourselves for your system
You terrorize us with your laws so we can obey

We work and work for the minimum wage
We work and work to the maximum stage
We work and work so you can enrich yourself

Criollo, I gotta love you!
Criollo, you gotta educate yourself!
Criollo, you have to put some truth in what you say
Criollo, you have to love me for what I am

I gotta love you
I gotta respect you
I gotta let you know your fallacies as I am not perfect myself

HAPPINESS AND HARMONY

Happiness and harmony are the foundation of my whole being
Comprehending and sustaining this mentality brings about peace
Loving is what we all need
Respect and caring about humanity will always help us to succeed

Selfishness will never be the key
Egocentrism will destroy you and me
We have to find a solution here
We have to eliminate hypocrisy to maintain this well-being

We must live as one in this community
We must defeat stereotypes and supremacy
'Cause you and I, my friends, are the children's destiny
'Cause you and I, brothers and sisters, are humanity

And we are never going to live in peace
If we don't turn over self-destruction into harmony and peace

HARMONY AND TRANQUILITY

My life is my sugar baby girl
My free will is changing my destiny, bro
My music is opening many doors,
My own poetry is rejoicing many souls

My love is found in my actions, bro
My good deeds are lifting up the poor
My own struggles are reflected in my poems,
My own tribulations connect me with the poor

Uprising is knocking on my door
A new beginning is giving me hope
Unification is shining for sure
Respect is giving us love

Let us plant this new message, bro
Let us grow this new seed among the poor
Let us harvest what we've planted, bro
Let us unite in one body and in one love

Let us shine through the darkness, bro
Let us become one people for sure
So we can live in harmony and tranquility, bro,
Among this beautiful people and upon this beautiful world

I AM A NATIVE MAN

I am a native man (my friends)!
I am a Mesoamerican!
I am not an alien (as some say)!
I am not a conqueror!

I am a humble man!
I am a poet!
I am a human being!
I am life's lover!

I will go and march for dignity!
I will go and find liberty!

I will resist and overcome this segregation!
I will upraise and establish emancipation!
I will write down the oppressed lamentations!
I will bring love, freedom, and resignation!

If my feet stumble today, Lord!
And my heart stops completely tonight!
Lift me up to Zion, Lord!
Carry me up to the promised land!
Set me free and wipe the tears from my eyes!

'Cause too many children are dying!
'Cause too many people are crying!
'Cause too many souls are fighting!
They are fighting and fighting among themselves!

I am dancing with the waves!
I am singing from my heart!
I am looking through reality!
I am praying to the Most High!

It is a beautiful day (my friends)!
It is a peaceful and relaxing day!
It is a wonderful day (my friends)!
It is an awesome and pleasant day!

Looking at the future to improve myself!
Looking at the past to identify ourselves!
Looking at the present to redeem my own mistakes!

The wind is blowing and blowing so gentle today!
The breeze is passing and passing on my way!
The light from the sun is shining and shining so bright!
The voice of freedom itself is given to all mankind!

I WILL REACH MOUNT ZION

I'm a freeman like the waters from the rain!
I'm a freeman like any other man!
I am a peacemaker and refuse to fight back!
I'm a humble man and only wish to remain alive!

But the rich keep on oppressing me with political laws!
The dominant culture terrorizes me with ideas of repatriation and
building a great wall!

But I am a Mesoamerican man
And have been resisting genocide and world domination
Since five hundred years ago!

I'm still segregated and alienated in my own land!
I'm still trapped in captivity in our motherland!

I remember my people in the mountains protecting their own lives!
I remember my native people being conquered and the genocide!
I remember my own self paying the same price!
I remember my people working in the fields and in the mines!
I remember my people dying because of this new system all this
time!

I used to run freely in my jungle before the conquerors arrived!
I used to live happily and freely in our motherland!

I now cry in my heart with tears of blood of the innocent ones!
I now cry in the fields and in the mines!
I now cry for the innocent people who didn't survive!
I now cry in the last days before this new system that is taking
many lives!

I am the target for supremacy and political laws!
I am the Almighty's child looking for acceptance and love in my
own land!

There is no room for hatred in my heart!
There is no room for revenge in my soul!
There is no room for lack of understanding in my mind!

And I will survive!
I will see the light!
I will reach Mount Zion now and in the future to come!
I will see the Almighty's holy temple with my own human eyes!

INVISIBLE SLAVE

I am the modern slave of this new era!
Chained with invisible regulations of immorality on both hands!
Defeated with rejections and hateful stereotypes
Upon the fields of endless grief pleading on my knees for death!

I am the existing zombie in the largest cemetery
Protector of the tombstones of my own people
Walking in this place of sorrow with no more tears
Disappointed of life and tired of struggling against this living
world!

I come from a far land of poverty and corruption
Where as much as I tried to hold my breath,
I ended up in a total anger explosion!

I flew like the eagle out of the desert to the mountains
To build my nest on the highest point of the rock,
Provide food for my empty stomach and feel protected

But the hunter captured my wind with his hands,
And placed me in a small golden cage segregated and rejected
I live in the same cycle of curse that my ancestors have created,
Where prayers for freedom have been never heard,
But only dreams exist that bring us hope for salvation,
And glory to go to heaven to receive holy purification

My masters are not just my forefathers' own blood,
But all the new generation around my naked soul
I am not just forced to follow the Ten Commandments,
But also the rules written in their own amendments

My destiny since my birth has been to suffer
And see my masters prosper and become even stronger
The dreams of changing the roots to my own direction
Are every time more confused and bizarre with no connection

I am segregated with partial rights
And humiliated on the media by politicians as a hateful crime
I am so disappointed of this society and so discontent
Upon the treasure of my masters' feet showing lament!

Freedom is what I claim every day
In my prayers and every night of my life
With the hope that someday
I will be able to practice my own will
And not my masters' lies!

I am the invisible slave of this confused land
Pleading on my knees for mercy with all my heart
So I can finally run away from my past
And see with my own human eyes
God's holy light!

JUSTICE

You are the answer to my human needs!
You bring sincerity, happiness, and love to me!
You bring recovery when I feel alone and sick!
You are my remedy when I'm feeling grief!

With you, I'm complete!
Without you, I'm empty within!
You bring me hope when I'm hopeless!
When I'm in agony, you set me free!

You are the perfect element that my body needs!
The perfect substance from the perfect being!
Your love is so addictive and so sweet!
You are my joy and my spiritual relief!
You are my sunshine and my harmony!

In my dreams, you are my possibilities!
In this sweet life, my personal rebirth!
You are duality, morality, equality, and rightfulness to me!
You are the rules of quality and conformity!
You are the equal balance of quantity!

—◦/◦/◦—

In our human laws, you are fairly, justly, and properly!
You are genuine and great peace to humanity!
In our whole world, you are harmony and peace!

You are the perfect element that my body needs!
The perfect substance from the perfect being!
Your love is so addictive and so sweet!
You are my joy and my spiritual relief!
You are my sunshine and my harmony!

In my dreams, you are my possibilities!
In this sweet life my personal rebirth!
You are duality, morality, equality, and rightfulness to me!
You are the rules of quality and conformity!
You are the equal balance of quantity!

In our human laws, you are fair, just, and proper!
You are genuine and great peace to humanity!
In our whole world, you are harmony and peace!

LET THE MUSIC STOP BIGGER MAN

Small Child won't attack Bigger Man!
Small Child won't be upraised unless is oppressed!

Small Child only wants to eat!
Small Child only wants to play!
Small Child wants to live in peace!
Small Child wants to be able to rest!

But Bigger Man is forcing him to kill another man!
Small Child doesn't want to obey!

'Cause Small Child only wants to eat!
'Cause Small Child only wants to play!
'Cause Small Child only wants to live in peace!
'Cause Small Child only wants to be able to rest!

But Bigger Man is forcing him to kill another man!
Small Child doesn't want to obey!

Don't let anyone confuse you with philosophical practices today!
Don't let anyone mislead you with information on TV by deceiving man!
Don't let anyone force you to kill another man!
Don't let anyone make you stumble and put you to shame!

'Cause Small Child only wants to eat!
'Cause Small Child only wants to play!
'Cause Small Child only wants to live in peace!
'Cause Small Child only wants to be able to rest!

But Bigger Man is forcing him to kill another man!
Small Child doesn't want to obey!

So let the music stop Bigger Man!
Let the love of Small Child be spread!
Let the sound of Small Child be heard!
Let genocide be stopped completely today!

LIBERTY

There is no one like you,
Who makes me feel all these feelings that I feel for you!
I cannot sleep!
Your presence is active in my memory!

It's the way you love me!
Your moral views and righteousness fully restore me!
It's your energy!
Your positive vibration motivates my whole being!

You are the perfect woman for me!
You will be my queen, and I will be your king!
Together we will rule the world!
We will love each other as it's supposed to be!
We will be a happy family!

I will be loving you!
And you will be loving me!
I will be protecting you!
And you will be protecting me!

Together forever as royalty!
There will be equality and duality!
You and me!
As equal beings in this society!

Love will rule our world!
Happiness will conquer our souls!
We will be in love!
Singing joyful songs!

We will be in peace!
All our elements will be in harmony!
Together you and me!
Establishing a better destiny!
Better opportunity!

We will make it last!
We'll forget the past!
We'll create a new future for us!

You will be my queen, and I will be your king!
Together we will rule the world!
We will love each other as it's supposed to be!
We will be a happy family!

I will be loving you!
And you will be loving me!
I will be protecting you!
And you will be protecting me!

—⟨۰/۰/۰⟩—

Together forever as royalty!
There will be equality and duality!
You and me!
As equal beings in this society!

Love will rule our world!
Happiness will conquer our souls!
We will be in love!
Singing joyful songs!

We will be in peace!
All our elements will be in harmony!
Together you and me!
Establishing a better destiny!
Better opportunity!

We will make it last!
We'll forget the past!

We'll create a new future for us!
We will reach the stars!
We will see the light!
We will finally unite for a better future to come

LOVE AND FAITH IN EXISTENCE

Life is beautiful to us!
Life is a blessing tonight!
The air we breathe is a blessing, brothers and sisters!
The songs we sing are a blessing for all mankind!

The mystery and the origin of time!
The diversity and complexity of life!
The superiority of many men toward us!

We were colonized!
We were minimized!
We worked in the fields and the mines!
We still work every day until the falling night!

We moved from place to place from time to time!
We go in exile to protect our lives!
We come back to the big cities to start a new life!
We come back to be accepted for who we are!

Love is the language to reunite!
Affection is the chemical that we all have—
To bring us together in harmony in this future time!

War is not the answer for human beings to survive!
Supremacy is not the mentality that keeps us alive!
But it is love and faith in existence within you and I!

Life is beautiful to us!
Life is a blessing tonight!
The air we breathe is a blessing, brothers and sisters!
The songs we sing are a blessing for all mankind!

Love is the language to reunite!
Affection is the chemical that we all have—
To bring us together in harmony in this future time!

War is not the answer for human beings to survive!
Supremacy is not the mentality that keeps us alive!
But it is love and faith in existence within you and I!

MAKE IT CHANGE

It's a beautiful day, my friends!
It's a beautiful and pleasant day!
It's a wonderful and chill day, my friends!
It's an awesome and gentle day

What's up with the world today?
What's up with this new system?
What's up with this new media?
What's up with this new music that is making us change in the
wrong way!

My life is more meaningful to me, brother!
My life is more meaningful to me, sister!
More meaningful than globalization and control!

My freedom is more valuable to me, brother!
My freedom is more valuable to me, sister!
More meaningful than power and laws!

Why do you oppress me today, dear friend?
Why do you exploit me every single day?
Why do you force us to feel depressed, dear friend?
Why do you force us to enslave ourselves?

Make it change, dear brother
Make it change!
Make it change, dear sister, make it change!

Because one day we will be upraised!
We will be upraised everywhere
We will be upraised,
And we'll free ourselves!

Because our life is more meaningful to us, dear sister!
More meaningful to us, dear brother!
More meaningful than silver and gold!

Because our freedom is more valuable to us, dear sister!
More valuable to us, dear brother!
More valuable to us than money and new clothes

Because there is nothing wrong with this place, dear friends!
There is nothing wrong!
But it is the mentality and the actions in it!

My life is more meaningful to me, brother!
My life is more meaningful to me, sister!
More meaningful than globalization and control!

My freedom is more valuable to me, brother!
My freedom is more valuable to me, sister!
More meaningful than power and laws!

Why do you oppress me today, dear friend?
Why do you exploit me every single day?
Why do you force us to feel depressed, dear friend?
Why do you force us to enslave ourselves?

Make it change, dear brother
Make it change!
Make it change, dear sister
Make it change!

Because one day we will be upraised!
We will be upraised everywhere
We will be upraised,
And we'll free ourselves!

Because our life is more meaningful to us, dear sister!
More meaningful to us, dear brother!
More meaningful than silver and gold!

Because our freedom is more valuable to us, dear sister!
More valuable to us, dear brother!
More valuable than money and new clothes!

Because there is nothing wrong with this place, dear friends!
There is nothing wrong!
But it is the mentality and the actions in it!

Cem Anáhuac
Tawantinsuyo

MAMA AMERICA

Mama America,
Land of my birth
Mama America,
I stand with my feet on the earth

You conquered my heart
You brought understanding to my mind
I'm not an alien, as some people believe that I am
I'm an Afro-Mestizo born as a new race

Your beauty is so easy to explain
Your loving is so natural to comprehend
I am a man who understands our past
Our present is our future, keep it in mind

My love is for the motherland
So beautiful is our wonderland
Mother Earth, I keep you in my heart
Love for all creation calls us to unite

Mama America,
Land of my birth
Mama America,
I stand with my feet on the earth

I need to love you like no one else
I need to take care of you in every single way
Every day is a brand-new day
I must show love to my fellow men

I'm the new race
There's no need to bring hatred to myself

Mama America,
Land of my birth
Mama America,
I stand with my feet on the earth

You're an outstanding flower blooming so great
The grace of the Creator is shining on your face
I didn't conquer or enslave my own self
I just brought unification with my special blend

Mama America,
Land of my birth
Mama America,
I stand with my feet on the earth

I cry on your feet for your dismay
All the blood spilled by your children will not be in vain
For all the women that were raped
I ask for forgiveness to my own myself

Forgive and forget
As we feed from your breast
Wipe the tears on your face
And provide us with our daily bread

Mama America,
Land of my birth
Mama America,
I stand with my feet on the earth

As indigenous people,
We'll reach success
We'll overcome inequality as inferior race
We will unite as children of the Maize

Mesoamerica will reign again
We will rewrite our own history as we stand
We will be the only survivors till the end

MESOAMERICA AND NORTE CHICO MUST UNITE

The Eagle and the Condor must unite as foretold in the ancient
prophecy
Mesoamericans and Norte Chico in South America must unite as
today's necessity!
Our history was erased from the Western civilization books!
Our existence was never written by the conquerors!

European languages were forced to be spoken!
Our indigenous languages and culture were replaced!
Our temples and cities were destroyed!
A new religion was introduced to keep us in control

A new economic system was brought to us
It gave them power over us, and it enslaved us!
It segregated us and alienated us!
Our land was stolen, and a new political system was established

We must rewrite our own history so we can survive and not perish!
We must unite and remain strong so we can finally flourish!
From Tierra del Fuego, Argentina, and Chile to Alaska!
Throughout the whole American continent!

From the Pacific Ocean to the east toward the Atlantic Ocean!
From a shining sea in the West Coast to the other shining sea in
the East Coast
And all in between!

We must spread the good news among ourselves!
There will be full equality and no more partiality everywhere!
The dominant culture will grant us the privilege to be successful!
We will be educated and remain prosperous!

We will be fruitful in our motherland and become grateful!
It will give us pride of being who we are as an indigenous people!
It will give us a place in this society to become equal!

It will establish duality, peace, and harmony among all creations.
It will help us to unified forces among all indigenous nations.
It will makes us understand the elements of life.
It will help us to protect them cautiously in order to survive.

It will allow us to see that water, oxygen, and earth bring us life.
It will teach our future generations to protect our own habitat.
It will help us to protect Mother Earth with our own lives.
It will allow us to unified humanity in the future to come.

MESOAMERICAN MAN

War takes lives!
Poor people die!
Rich become richer
To control our lives!

Unknown time! Unknown future!
Mesoamerican man
Knows his own culture!
We were colonized!

Some others died!
Some us survived!
Some others stayed!
And some others fled to the mountains!

Mesoamericans taken in captivity!
Native men forced into slavery!
Long hours of hard labor!
Long years in segregation!

Division among our tribes!
Hatred killing many lives!
Exploitation upon mankind!
Alienation in my own land!

Crying in my heart!
Extermination upon my own kind!

Working every day!
Working for the minimum wage!
Enslaving myself!
Working to the maximum stage!

Water from the sky!
Water on my eyes!
Water on the ocean!
Water on the rivers!
Water for all mankind!

Second-class North American citizen is what I am!
Dehumanizing by this new system every day!
Resisting persecution along the way!
Crying for justice, on my knees I pray!

Human race,
We need to unite!
Native men,
We need to survive!

Let's redeem the events from the past!
Let's overcome any genocide!
Respect and acceptance are the key!
Love and unification will help us to succeed!

Let's overcome this little trouble!
Let's help each other in our own struggles!
Let this human race hear us out!
Let them understand our suffering now!

We don't need any more trouble!
We don't need any more sorrow!
We don't need any more alienation!
We only need acceptance and unification!

MESTIZA (LIGHT-BROWN-SKINNED GIRL)

My mind is lost in this feeling!
Insomnia came into my life!
My heart is hoping and willing,
Tonight your kisses were mine!

Long time confused in this feeling
Long time wishing to see your eyes!
This life to me is meaningless,
This loneliness is oppressing my life!

Crying for my love
(Crying for my life)
Crying for my babe
(Crying tonight)

Things are not the way we want
It's hurting
(It's hurting, darling)
It' hurting deep inside

O sweet mestiza,
My beautiful European and Mesoamerican blood!

Keep on knocking the doors for unity!
Keep on knocking the doors for equality!
Keep on knocking the doors for me!
Keep on feeding me with positive energy!
Keep on targeting me!

Don't feel confused!
Don't feel divided!
Don't hate yourself!

Free yourself!
Love yourself!
Be yourself!
Be amazed!

Be the footsteps of what it will be!
Be the example of what it is supposed to be!
Be the reason for unity and for equality!
Be the best that you can be!

Be the queen!
Be my chick!
Be the future to be!
Be the role model of the perfect dream!

Be the royal existence of my own fantasies!
Be the perfect being!
Be the blended genes of today's society!
Be the creation of this reality!

Be the perfect example of humanity!
You and me fighting along each other for full equality!
Conquering stereotypes and vanity!
Establishing opportunities for what tomorrow will bring!

We have defeated supremacy!
We have created integrity!
We have understood about this necessity!
We are the perfect roots for this society!

We represent all humanity!
We want to create a better way for unity!
We want to change our destiny!
We want to set ourselves free!

We want to think critically!
We want to educate our community!
We want to give people the key to this philosophy!
We want people to truly see what love can bring!

MOTHER EARTH NEEDS TO SURVIVE

Mother Earth, I have you in me
Mother Nature, you're part of my being
You must live so I can live
You keep me alive and complete

As I sit on my balcony and dream
I think constantly about you and me
You always set my mind and my spirit free
You give me shelter and company

You are the key to my heart
You are the breath to my soul
You are the hope to my mind
You give me company when I'm alone

I see the light in your eyes
I taste the sweetness in my mouth
You have what my heart desires
You satisfy everything mile per mile

You are the roots to my love
You are the oxygen to my lungs
You keep my heart pumping
You circulate in my own blood

Mother Earth, I have you in me
Mother Nature, you're part of my being
You must live so I can live
You keep me alive and complete

I am your child and your offspring
I see the mountains and the trees
I see the ocean and feel the breeze
I see the cities and the human beings

Your destruction I will never permit
I will defend you with everything in me
I will save you with my own deeds
I will protect you from any human being

You give us shelter
You give us food
You give us oxygen
You give us a roof

I cannot allow to see you destroyed
I have to protect you and give you love
I have to inform people and let them know
We are destroying our own selves

Corporations cannot think for ourselves
We have to get out of our shells
We have to stand up to prevail
We have to fight back for ourselves

Fight back is the plan
Save our home to survive
It's for our children that we're fighting back
For a better place and a better future to come

MOVING AND GROOVING

Plants, herbs, and tropical trees!
Mountains, valleys, and the ocean breeze!
Tropical music is playing on the beach!
Playing so nice that makes you wanna move your hips!

The moon and the stars are shining so bright!
The waves are moving with the ocean tides!
Birds are singing and flying in the sky!
Smoking ganja in the open relaxes my mind!

You could see it in my eyes!
Happiness reflected from deep in my heart!
Drumbeats are playing so loud!
Smoke is arising in a foggy cloud!

People come together to see us play!
Laughing and dancing is everywhere!
Drinking beer in the heat to cool down our sweat!
Passing a joint with people that we just met

No police is harassing in this open place!
People are moving and grooving from every race!
Nowhere else than this paradise would people rather stay!

Let the party begin!
People are moving their feet!
Music is playing so sweet!
Drums are playing in a cool beat!

Rhythm is coming out of me!
Rhymes are chanting poetry!

The sun is arising,
And we're still here!
The birds keep on singing—
In the sweetest melody!

We hug and kiss as we say goodbye!
Good vibes as we go away in the morning time!
Time to feel pleased in this paradise!
Time to say goodbye and be pleased on this day to come!

MUJER (LITTLE WOMAN)

Baby, I need your love!
Girl, I love you so!
Baby, I lose control!
Girl, I love you more!

In this times of isolation!
In these times of lamentations!
In these times of meditations!
In these times of reflections!

I need your company and love!
You might be gone,
But these lines made up a song!

I miss you and think about you in this love poem!
I write about you and lose control!
Girl, I miss you!

This is definitely true love!
So we go along
Loving each other through the whole world
Of imagination and hope!
Holding our feelings deep in our soul!

You love me, and I love you so!
You are my boo, and I am your man!

Not stressing ourselves!
Loving ourselves like crazy every single day!
You are the seed for humanity!
You are like the queen of a honeybee!

Without you, we do not exist!
With you, our survival exceeds!
You bring reproduction to society!
You bring about human beings!

Your love is so unique!
Your affection is so extreme!
I have so much love to give!
You are something to be thankful for—
That's what you mean to me!

I want to kiss you softly!
Keep you in my memory!
You are definitely in my dreams!
Little woman, thank you for being part of my reality!

When I'm alone, you set me free!
When I'm feeling hopeless, you bring hope to me!
You deserve to be my queen!

Little woman, I'll tell you this,
Eres la razon de mi existencia!
Eres la razon de mi existir!
Eres lo mas sagrado de la vida!
Eres el motivo de nuestro existir!

Sin ti nuestra existencia para de existir!
Con tu presencia logramos sobrevivir!
Tu eres el fruto, la semilla que llevo dentro de mi!
El futuro, el pasado y el presente por venir!
Una vez mas te lo digo: Eres la razon de mi vivir!

Eres el motivo de nuestro existir!
Con tu presencia logramos sobrevivir!
Tu eres el fruto, la semilla que llevo dentro de mi!
El futuro, el pasado y el presente por venir!

MY MUSIC

My life
Is the only thing I have!
My happiness
Is the most precious thing in my life!

I write to the sky!
I write to the ocean!
I write to the earth!
I write to my babe!
I write to express my emotions

I dance to my music
I dance to my music, man!
I dance to the music
The music coming from the oppressed!

Let me dance to my music
(Let me play!)
Let me jam to my music
(One day!)

Let me enjoy myself!
Let me enjoy this music with you today!
Let me chill with you someday!
Let me share the music coming from the oppressed!

My soul is hungry for peace!
My heart is thirsty for love!
In these times of suffering
(We gotta be strong!)

No nationalism will control our mind!
No patriotism will force us to take someone's life!

The feeling is so nice!
The moment is so fine!
The time is so lasting like the first time!

The sugar in your lips, honey,
Is so special to me!
The tenderness on your body, darling,
Keeps me company!

O beautiful morning!
O beautiful evening!
O beautiful time with you
(With lots of grace and thanksgiving!)

No crying!
No deceiving!
No suffering, brothers and sisters,
Is the way I'm living!

I'm resting my heart and mind!
I'm resting my feet tonight!
I'm finding the meaning
(The beautiful meaning!)
The meaning of life!
I'm finding understanding to the things to come!

I wanna be free like the rivers and the trees!
I wanna be happy like a flying bird!
I wanna be loved, baby, and be accepted as a human being!

Don't trouble yourself with vanity and fame!
Don't trouble yourself with hostility and domain!
Don't trouble yourself ever again!
Don't trouble yourself with tears and chronic pain!

MY NUMBER ONE

My soul sings spiritual poetry
Thinking freely about love and everything!
Feeling sympathy on everyone's tragedy!
Loving myself and others completely!

Creating my own destiny!
Looking for a new strategy to find love in this reality!
So many fantasies on my mind leaving me extremely happy!
Using creativity to create poetry!

Expressing myself through thoughtful writings!
Making rhymes to talk about everything!

Babe, you are my number one!
Out of all the girls, you are the one I want!

I want to express my feelings through many rhymes!
I want to touch your heart!
I want to fly to heaven and then come back!
I want to grab a star and put it on your hands!
I want to see the light!
I want to rock your world so many times!

Because, babe, you are my number one!
Because darling, you are the one I want!
You are the one my heart desires to share my life!
You are the one I love because you make me feel so alive!
You are the one I die for and breathe for—keep it in your mind!

Dejaria mi marca de besos por todas partes de tu cuerpo
Seria aprobado por los sentimientos de tu corazón
Llegaría profundamente hasta el fondo de tu alma
Permanecerá ahí por siempre y para siempre junto a ti
Para cuidarte y para amarte toda la vida y hasta el fin!

Because you are my number one, baby!
Because you are the one I want, honey!
You are the one my heart desires to share my life!
You are the one I love because you make me feel so alive!
You are the one I die for and breathe for—keep it in your mind!

Dejaria mi marca de besos por todas partes de tu cuerpo
Seria aprobado por los sentimientos de tu corazón
Llegaría profundamente hasta el fondo de tu alma
Permanecerá ahí por siempre y para siempre junto a ti
Para cuidarte y para amarte toda la vida y hasta el fin!

Y es verdad que dejaria mi marca de besos por todas partes de tu cuerpo
Y seria aprobado por los sentimientos de tu corazón
Y es verdad que llegaría profundamente hasta el fondo de tu alma
Permanesiendo ahí por siempre y para siempre junto a ti
Para cuidarte y para amarte toda la vida y hasta el fin!

Y te lo digo una vez mas:
"Dejaria mi marca de besos por todas partes de tu cuerpo
Seria aprobado por los sentimientos de tu corazón
Llegaría profundamente hasta el fondo de tu alma
Permanecerá ahí por siempre y para siempre junto a ti
Para cuidarte y para amarte toda la vida y hasta el fin!"

NARCO GOVERNMENT

Killing and operating in the name of the narco-government
Systematic corruption and homicidal moments
Oppressing the oppressed everywhere without you even knowing it
Forcing the common people to leave their belongings

Land and liberty were Zapata's last words of precious knowledge
Rebel since day one of my birth in my own country
Fighting globalization and private property against the first world
government

I am a soldier in this proletarian society
I am the survivor of this marginalized community
I am an observant creating good poetry
I am the victim of this political-economical bureaucracy

Land and liberty were Zapata's last words of precious knowledge
I am a rebel since day one of my birth in my own country
I've been fighting globalization and private property against this
first world government
I am a soldier in this proletarian society

I am the survivor of this marginalized community
I am an observant creating good poetry
I am the victim of this political-economical bureaucracy

ONE LOVING JAM

I'm living my time!
I'm living my life!
I'm living the moment!
I'm thinking about you tonight!

Sometimes I cry!
Sometimes I laugh!
Sometimes I smile!
Sometimes I feel love deep inside!

The sky is so blue!
The weather is so sweet!
My spirit is so strong!
My heart is in peace!

I'm getting up with the rising sun!
I'm waking up the feelings inside!
I'm leaving everything aside!
I'm thinking about you, babe, with a peaceful mind!

Tu cuerpo esta lleno de puesia!
Tu voz mi nena me llena de alegria!
Tu presencia es aliento a mi vida!
Tu perfume me acompaña día tras día!

—⟨∘⟩—

Que bien me siento cuando estoy contigo!
Que bien me siento cuando estas conmigo!

Las luces de los cielos se neutralizan!
Las aguas de los mares se tranquilizan!
Las fuerzas de los vientos se normalizan!
Las pupilas de mis ojos se regocijan!

Eres tan bella y tan hermosa!
Eres tan linda como una rosa!
Eres tan buena y tan preciosa!
Eres mas dulce que la miel de tu boca!

No more confusion!
No more isolation!
No more feeling down!
No more lamentations!

One loving jam for you, babe
(One loving jam!)
One loving jam for my brothers and sisters
(One loving jam!)

One loving jam for my neighbors
(One loving jam!)
One loving jam for myself
(One loving jam!)
One loving jam for the Most High
(One loving jam!)

Because I'm living my time, babe!
Because I'm living my life!
Because I'm living the moment, honey!
Because I'm thinking about you tonight!

Sometimes I cry!
Sometimes I laugh!
Sometimes I smile!
Sometimes I feel love deep inside!

The sky is so blue!
The weather is so sweet!
My spirit is so strong!
My heart is in peace!

I'm getting up with the rising sun!
I'm waking up the feelings inside!
I'm leaving everything aside!
I'm thinking about you, babe, with a peaceful mind!

YOU ARE BEAUTIFUL

You are beautiful, as perfect as it sounds
A unique blooming flower attached to the ground
Your face is like a rose petal, so smooth and so fragile
That only my lips can touch and discover your hidden flavor

The soil that supports your being must have been taken from holy ground
From up there on the mountains where the Lord has his dwelling house
The roots that hold your feet are so deep and so strong
Restoring my broken soul from all the pain of this world

The vivid color of life that surrounds your body
Moves so gently from one place to the other
The light of your smile is so bright and so warm
Reflecting purity upon the darkest side of my life

You are an angel from heaven who brings me the light
Restoring my human body, my soul, and my broken heart
Your voice is like a hymn to my ears
An angelic peaceful song of love for my eyes to see

You are as beautiful as the sunlight on the sea
When the wind moves the breeze so gently to the beach
Your enormous happiness overcomes every angle of my life
Fulfilling all my needs with just the look of your eyes

Your enchanting magic hypnotizes my whole body
Making my whole body dance in an underground party
The grace upon your face is so intense and so special
Making me travel in a trance to another dimension

I will look for your smile among this confused world
And will never rest my feet until I conquer your love
I want to kiss you with the same passion of love, forever, girl,
And declare with my lips that I still love you so

I want to live together with you in our lovely home
And love you madly with all my heart and soul

You are so beautiful,
As perfect as it sounds
My inspiration of love,
The strength of my soul

The phrases on this poem,
Written on this song
And the only reason
That keeps my feet on the ground.

OUR MOTHERLAND

You face is so beautiful!
Your lips are so sweet!
Your love is so intense!
Your smile is so unique!

This moment is so perfect!
Our feelings are so real!
This passion is so truthful!
If you want me to prove it for God, I will!

You give me shelter when sadness comes!
You give me company when loneliness arrives!
You give me love and positive vibes!
You give me so much passion in our quality time!

I'm so glad, so glad to be alive!
I'm so happy, so happy in my life!
I'm so grateful, so grateful inside!
I'm so thankful, so thankful to the Most High!

Mi corazón es como una flor!
Tu cuerpo es como una rosa!
Mi canto es como una expresión—
De una manera tan hermosa!

I will worship the Almighty with all my strength!
I will worship the Creator with all my heart!
I will sing for freedom and redemption for us!
I will plead for mercy and justice for all mankind!

Mi Mestiza, Mi Mulata, Mi Samba
y Mi Costeña de este Paraiso Tropical!
Tus raíces llevan historia ancestral!
Eres la semilla mística que nos hace vibrar!
Tu existencia lleva motivos de igualdad!

I'm so happy to have been born in the motherland!
Mesoamerica!
Roots of my future, present, and past!

No more border lines!
No more division among our native tribes!
No more genocide!

Engraving our history in our own hearts!
Rewriting our own reality on these lines!
Emancipating five hundred years of suppression in our own land!

PEACE AROUND THE WORLD

My heart is scrambling for peace
My soul is thirsty for love
Long-suffering I have seen
In these times of war, brothers and sisters our children deserve to live

There is no reason to genocide
There is no reason to bow down our heads and cry
Humanity deserves to live
Hatred must come down to our feet

Unification among mankind
Redemption within our path
Will bring prosperity in these hard times

Love is the answer to our everyday cry
Love is the key
To unify humanity's well-being

We must look for this missing link
We must find happiness within
'Cause humanity is me, brothers and sisters
'Cause humanity is you
'Cause humanity must unite to bring prosperity and peace!

REACHING OUT TO PEOPLE'S HEARTS

The Santa Ana winds are blowing
Tears from my eyes are rolling
The leaves from the trees are falling
My mind is thinking about our loving

I'm surviving in this daily competition
Keeping control and resisting is my mission
Respecting and keeping on mind this decision
Finding love and acceptance is my vision

I've been rejected so much in my path
I've been unwanted and hated in life
But I still love people for who they are
I'm still on my feet, happy to be alive

Xenophobia won't keep me down
Brown is beautiful, I'm telling you now
I've got native roots no doubt
I got pride and my feet on the ground

Standing up against injustices
Fighting back in the search for justice
The dominant society against just us
Waiting on you to begin to trust us

Standing up for all humanity
Uprising among this society
Searching for full equality
Peace and love is our main mentality

Creating new strategies to reach people's love
Eliminating any hatred around the world
Looking through humanity to bring us close
Thinking of new ways that will benefit many of us

Love is the key for unification
Hatred will only bring more corruption
Forgive and forget is the way through redemption
Full equality will benefit this beautiful nation

Humankind must love itself and unite
Human race must uprise and fight back
This understanding must help us to see the light
Indigenous people must get together and survive.

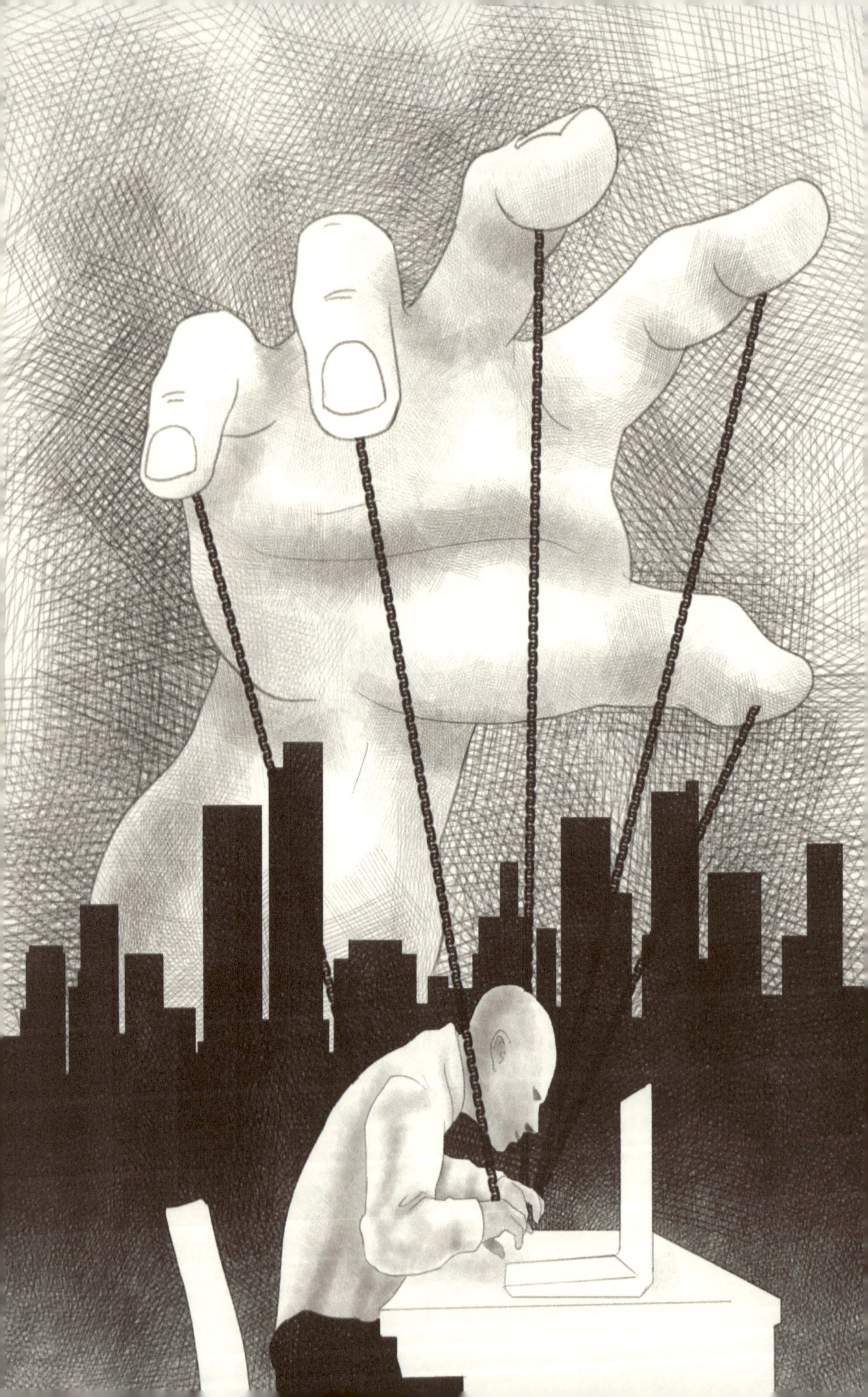

RESISTING MODERN SLAVERY

It's the pressure, babe
(It's the pressure!)
It's the pressure that society is putting us on!

It's the rules and regulations, honey
(It's the rules and regulations!)
It's the rules and regulations that are forcing us to be controlled!

So I keep myself alert and moving on!
I keep resisting this socioeconomic system all along!
I keep on moving forward, darling!

I keep on resisting modern slavery, honey
(I keep on living my life for this long!)
It's just this pressure, babe
(It's just this pressure!)
It's just this pressure that's bugging me on!

Time is knocking on our door, honey
(Time is knocking on our door!)
Time is knocking on our door to freedom coming for the poor!

I stop for a moment,
And my boss says, "Work!"
I try my best to perform,
And my boss still says, "Work!"

I compete with everyone else, darling!
And I still have not reached a comfortable economic growth!

It's the pressure, babe
(It's the pressure!)
It's the pressure that society is putting us on!

It's the rules and regulations, honey
(It's the rules and regulations!)
It's the rules and regulations that are forcing us to be controlled!

So I keep myself alert and moving on!
I keep resisting this socioeconomic system all along!
I keep on moving forward, darling!

I keep on resisting modern slavery, honey
(I keep on living my life for this long!)
It's just this pressure, babe
(It's just this pressure!)
It's just this pressure that's bugging me on!

Time is knocking our door, honey
(Time is knocking our door!)
Time is knocking on our door to freedom coming for the poor!

I stop for a moment,
And my boss says, "Work!"
I try my best to perform,
And my boss still says, "Work!"

I compete with everyone else, darling!
And I still have not reached a comfortable economic growth!

ROSE (SAMBA)

The music is playing
It's playing, babe
It's playing on the ocean waves tonight!

The breeze is refreshing
Is refreshing my mind!

My tears are falling down
Falling down, honey,
Falling down among the salty sand!

The stars are shining so bright!
The ocean waves are singing to my heart!
In the darkness, I sit alone and cry!

This way I sing praises
I sing praises, darling
I sing praises to the Most High!

You are the center of my universe!
My summer during my winter days!
The sound of this phrase!
Poetry itself!
The oxygen of my very lasting breath!

Yes, babe, you heard me!
You are the sun, the stars, and the galaxy!
You are my queen!
And in my to-do list, you are priority!

In the whole world,
You are my everything!
Nothing else matters to me!
You are my freedom within

Money means nothing to me!
True happiness is what we all need!
A good education on every single kid!
It's the foundation to overcome any remaining grief!

Equality!
No partiality!
It's what we all need!

Rose samba,
Fresh flower!
Dynamite power!
Music coming from my soul

Heartbeat!
Lovely and unique!
Roots of an evergreen tree!
Rhythm coming out of me!

Crying of joy!
Together one love!
In one song!
Flowing around the world

The stars are shining so bright!
The ocean waves are singing to my heart!
In the darkness, I sit alone and cry!

This way I sing praises
I sing praises, darling
I sing praises to the Most High!

You are the center of my universe!
My summer during my winter days!
The sound of this phrase!
Poetry itself!

The oxygen of my very lasting breath!
You are the sun, the stars, and the galaxy!
You are my queen!
And in my to-do list, you are priority!

In the whole world,
You are my everything!
Nothing else matters to me!
You are my freedom within

Money means nothing to me!
True happiness is what we all need!
A good education on every single kid!
It's the foundation to overcome any remaining grief!

Equality!
No partiality!
It's what we all need!

Rose samba,
Fresh flower!
Dynamite power!
Music coming from my soul

Heartbeat!
Lovely and unique!
Roots of an evergreen tree!
Rhythm coming out of me!

Crying of joy!
Together one love!
In one song!
Flowing around the world

SETTING MYSELF FREE (A NEW PSALM)

Brother, why do you terrorize us with political laws?
Sister, why do you feel xenophobic against us?
Why do you use your immigration system to keep us in control?
Why do you separate us with that border wall?

We've been working for your system for all this long
We've been enslaving ourselves since five hundred years ago
Give us a hand
We deserve a new change
We deserve to be fruitful in our own land

We've been always there
Throughout history, we've been always oppressed
Since the arrival of this new system,
We've been always depressed

We enslave ourselves every single day
We try to survive in every single way
It is too much pressure that we cannot sustain
We have to take a break

From this reality,
We have to free ourselves
There has to be a better way
A better place to release ourselves

O tears are falling down my eyes, brother
I need to see the light
I need to set myself free, sister
I need to survive

I need to reach the sky
I need to enter into paradise
I need to have the strength to not getting stuck
I need to forget the past

I need to follow a new plan
I need to maintain strong until trouble passes by
This is my new psalm
This is the voice of the voiceless praying to the Most High

I alone pay the price
I alone will survive
I alone will make it change
With this poetry and these rhymes

You need to hear this truth
You need to hear this cry
You need to send us love and respect
In this future to come

SINCERITY WILL BRING ABOUT HARMONY

Life is beautiful,
I always tell myself
Life is wonderful
When everything is in harmony within ourselves

The stars, the ocean, and the winds
Are the elements that fulfill this happiness in me
The mountains, the hills, and the valleys
Are great places on this earth—
That I love very madly

Love is the greatest precious thing
Peacefulness eliminates any grief
Poetry is obviously coming out of me
Creativity is building great phrases right here
'Cause sincerity, my friends, is restoring my disturbed heart into
one piece!

SOCIAL CHANGE

Brothers and sisters are dying everywhere
Brothers and sisters need some shelter and help
Hunger is spreading among the poor
A new uprising will be arising and born

The rich must listen to this call
The wealthy must listen to the crying from our soul
Now is the moment to reunite
Now is the moment to eliminate corruption and crime

A new social change will be pulled out and born
A better opportunity will help out the poor
Come and join us together in one love
Come out, brothers and sisters, be happy and rejoice

Don't let the past ruin your present, bro
Don't let the present ruin your future, bro
Don't let your ego destroy this feeling inside
Don't let your vanity be suppressing your heart

'Cause now is the time, brother man
Now is the time
To show appreciation and thanksgiving to mankind

SPEAK UP AND STAND UP FOR YOUR RIGHTS

Brother, rise up
Sister, speak up
Everyone, stand up
And exercise your rights

Don't keep your mouth shut
Say it aloud
Full equality is for every child
Every human being no matter what

No matter the color of the skin
No matter what country you live in
Nor a place in society
We all deserve to live equally free

No matter what gender and age
Nor religion you believe in
In the eyes of the Almighty,
We're all His children

No matter how rich you might be
No matter how poor you might be
We all have the same opportunity to succeed

Corruption is not the key
Love is the key
To lift up everyone in society

No matter how healthy you might be
No matter how sick you might be
The right to live in peace is the best remedy

Brother, rise up
Sister, speak up
Everyone, stand up
And exercise your rights

It's in the Book of Life
We must love and unite
We must see the light
We must reach full equality in the future to come

It is humane not to take this in vain
The Almighty will heal all the pain
There's no need to be stressed
After the storm, we must love the rain

The human race will find new ways
Against climate catastrophes
We must keep this in our heads
The solution is out there waiting for ourselves

It is the indigenous people's ways
Protecting Mother Earth
Against the human race
The solution is in ourselves

Don't be in silence
Speak up your truth
No matter the cause
You must fight for it

Brother, rise up
Sister, speak up
Everyone, stand up
And exercise your rights

THE TRUTH IS WITHIN YOURSELF

Don't believe in anything people tell you!
Don't believe in anything they might say!
If you ever want to know the truth,
The truth is within yourself!

Find the truth to your questions!
Find the answer to your dismay!
Look into the Book of Life and free yourself!

People only tell you the truth in half ways!
People only tell you to follow their own fate!

But don't let anyone deceive you!
Don't let anyone control your blessings today!
For no one knows your desires to finding the righteous way!

Be always skeptical and always alert!
Be always devoted and always willing to learn!
For the truth is the light of your faith!
For the truth is the life of your strength!

So don't be wicked and be afraid!
For the truth is found within yourself!
To give you directions and show you the way!

THIS BEAUTIFUL MUSIC

Oh, beautiful morning,
Oh, beautiful night!
Oh, beautiful ocean,
Oh, beautiful stars

Oh, beautiful music
Oh, yeah—
Oh, beautiful sunshine!

Don't let these feelings drift away from your heart
Don't let this music stop for a moment tonight!
Don't let the weather make you sad!
Don't let any agony strike you deep inside

The rain is coming, but it won't last
The storm is arriving, but we'll be fine
Those sweet moments are coming to pass
The cold is here, but it's all right

'Cause there is a beautiful morning coming up
'Cause this is a beautiful night
'Cause there is a beautiful ocean rising up
'Cause there are some beautiful stars

'Cause there comes this beautiful music with the high tides
O yeah, quenching and fulfilling my heart
I said, there comes this beautiful music with the high tides—
Scaring all the fear and sadness (before the sunshine)!

WE HAVE A MORAL JOB TO DO

I'm alone in this awesome place thinking about my love!
I'm alone trying to write a peaceful song!
I'm alone in this mellow mood praying to the Lord my love!

'Cause I've seen so many things in this world!
And don't want to die without writing a peaceful song!

How can I explain this truth to my people!
How can I confess our sinful deeds to the people without creating a
war!

Please Lord, don't judge me, no!
Don't leave me, no!
Don't take away this great peace from my soul!

'Cause I've seen so many things in this world!
And don't want to die without writing a peaceful song!

I'm walking through the night!
I'm walking towards the light!
Please don't let any evil defeat me tonight!

'Cause I'm feeling good in this righteous path!
'Cause I'm feeling fine in this awesome night!
But there is a lot of work to be done, my love!
To satisfy all the needs and wants of all mankind!

Class, gender, and race have always affected this human race!
Love, morality, and truth are always suppressed by immoral views!
Whoever is oppressed has all the right to be upraised!
Whoever is enslaved has all the choices to fight back!

It is all rational, man, don't confuse yourself!
The world goes around and around!
While we are hating and destroying ourselves!
There is still a lot of work to be done in this life!

There is still a lot of inequality among mankind!
So we have a job to do, my love!
We have a moral job to do in this life!
To finally be able to satisfy all the needs and wants of all mankind!

We have a moral job to do in this life!
We have a job to do in this righteous path!
To satisfy all the needs and wants for all mankind!

'Cause I'm feeling good in this righteous path!
'Cause I'm feeling fine in awesome night!
But there is a lot of work to be done, my love!
To satisfy all the needs and wants for all mankind!

Class, gender, and race have always affected this human race!
Love, morality, and truth are always suppressed by immoral views!
Whoever is oppressed has all the right to be upraised!
Whoever is enslaved has all the choices to fight back!

It is all rational, man, don't confuse yourself!
The world goes around and around!
While we are hating and destroying ourselves!

There is still a lot of work to be done in this life!
There is still a lot of inequality among mankind!
So we have a job to do, my love!
We have a moral job to do in this life!

To finally be able to satisfy all the needs and wants for all
mankind!
We have a moral job to do in this life!
We have a job to do in this righteous path!
To satisfy all the needs and wants for all mankind!

WE HAVE TO REUNITE OUR LOVING

Here I am behind this palm tree!
Here I am missing you, babe!
Here I am resting my feet!
Here I am singing love songs to you, honey!
Here I am wondering if you too miss me!

I'm loving the time I spend thinking about you!
I love you, boo
(I love you for sure!)
I love your sweet smile
(I love making love to you!)

You always get me in a good mood!
You always bring satisfaction too!

I could see the moon up in the sky!
I could see the stars shining so bright!
I always keep you on my mind
(So close to my heart!)

It's a wonderful feeling of joy in this life!
Times are sometimes hard!
Time is just a passing stage on this sweet life!
The Creator will provide!

The Almighty will show us the light at the proper time!
So show love to the people who love you the most!
Show appreciation to all creation in this life!
Show love and affection to all mankind!

We are the people of tomorrow!
We have to heal any remaining sorrow!
We have to survive in this daily competition!
We have to reunite our loving as a new mission!
We have to emancipate ourselves from any hatred!
We have to bring together humanity from all places!

'Cause harmony can kill so much pain!
'Cause working together can heal this confusion in our heads!
'Cause unification can bring full equality!
'Cause acceptance can bring us realistic duality!

I could see the moon up in the sky!
I could see the stars shining so bright!
I always keep you on my mind
(So close to my heart!)

It's a wonderful feeling of joy in this life!
Times are sometimes hard!
Time is just a passing stage of this sweet life!
The Creator will provide!

The Almighty will show us the light at the proper time!
So show love to the people who love you the most!
Show appreciation to all creation in this life!
Show love and affection to all mankind!

WE WILL UNITE

Let's give it up for the earth and the sky!
Let's give it up for the ocean and the mountainside!
Let's give it up for this human race and the plants!
Let's give it up for these peaceful moments tonight!

Our tribulations have faded away!
Our confrontations have ceased today!
No politician will make it change!
No supremacy will defeat us again!

We will unite, my friends
(We will unite)
As one people and one human race!

The time is fine with the moon and the stars!
Do you feel it, babe?
It's the breath in you and I!

There are solutions for every problem tonight!
Do you know that, honey?
So leave everything behind!
There is no need to cry in this beautiful life!

Time goes by so smooth and so gentle tonight!
So hold me tight, darling
Hold me tight!
It feels so good, babe
(It feels so good!)

So leave everything behind!
My love is for you, babe
(My love is for you!)
My affection is for you, honey
(My affection is for you!)
My life is for you, darling
(My life is for you!)
My time is for you, girl
(My time is for you!)
And only for you!

All we need is some music, babe!
All we need is the ocean, honey!
All we need is the moon, the sky, and the shining stars!
All we need is full equality in our own land!

How can you deny
This natural beauty given to us!
How can you be so blind
To deny true happiness to the starving people on the slums!

IT RAINS

It rains, babe
(It rains!)
It rains across the earth, honey
(It rains!)

It rains across the ocean, darling
(It rains!)
It rains blessings
(It rains!)
It rains upon mankind!
It rains, babe
(It rains!)

It rains among our history!
It rains upon our species!
It rains within our eyes!
It rains upon our lives!
It rains within our soul!
It rains blessings from the Most High!

No supremacy will defeat us again!
No politician will make it change!
We will unite, my friends
(We will unite)
As one people and one human race!

It rains across the earth, honey
(It rains!)
It rains across the ocean, darling
(It rains!)
It rains blessings
(It rains!)
It rains upon mankind!
It rains, babe
(It rains!)

It rains among our history!
It rains upon our species!
It rains within our eyes!
It rains upon our lives!
It rains within our soul!
It rains blessings from the Most High!

WHEN I DREAM

I'm free to run like the rivers from the mountains to the sea!
I'm free to fly like the birds from tree to tree!
I'm able to relax my feet!
I'm able to find peace within me!

Because I see you in my dreams!
Because I have you next to me!
Because I still have your love in my memory!

Sometimes I feel scared like a newborn child!
Sometimes I feel hurt like a good soldier in battle!
Sometimes I feel like I am able to reach the clouds!
Sometimes I feel like I am able to see your smile when I dream!

Here I come with a humble heart!
Here I go with happiness and love!
I don't need to mourn when I feel alone!
I don't need to cry when I feel sad!

When I think critically,
I am able to understand what we all need!
When I breathe gently,
I'm able to see myself accepted by this community!

But sometimes I feel scared like a newborn child!
Sometimes I feel hurt like a good soldier in battle!
Sometimes I feel like I am able to reach the clouds!
Sometimes I feel like I am able to see your smile when I dream!

And here I come with a humble heart!
Here I go with happiness and love!
I don't need to mourn when I feel alone!
I don't need to cry when I feel sad!

When I dream,
My life is complete!
When I think critically,
I am able to understand what we all need!
When I breathe gently,
I'm able to see myself accepted by this community!

WRITE ABOUT MY HISTORY

Loving, babe, is my way of life!
Loving, honey, is the way I survive!
Harmony between you and I!
Brings prosperity in this harvest time!
Love, babe, is what I give!
Love, honey, is what we all need!

In these times of suffering, darling
Do you hear me?
O can you see!

I won't fight against my brothers!
I will teach my people to love one another!
I will love my sisters with honor!
I will treat my babe as my only lover!

Because loving, babe, is my way of life!
Because loving, honey, is the way I survive!
Harmony between you and I!
Brings prosperity in this harvest time!
Love, babe, is what I give!
Love, honey, is what we all need!

In these times of suffering, darling
Do you hear me?
O can you see!

I won't fight against my brothers!
I will teach my people to love one another!
I will love my sisters with honor!
I will treat my babe as my only lover!

Write about these feelings, man!
Write about the oppressed!
Write about my history, man!
Write about the reason
(The reason)
The reason I'm feeling depressed!

I am the poor, brothers and sisters!
The poor…still…alive!
I am this poetry, brothers and sisters!
This poetry…written…on these lines!

I'm the oppressed searching for a new life
I am humanity ready to be upraised

Write about these good feelings about me, man
Give me the equality that I need
Don't spread xenophobia like disease
Give me full equality so I can live in peace

I want to be happy and in harmony
I want to be the best man that I can be
But if you build a wall around me,
I'll be miserable throughout history

Loving, babe, is my way of life!
Loving, honey, is the way I survive!
Harmony between you and I!
Brings prosperity in this harvest time!

Love, babe, is what I give!
Love, honey, is what we all need!

In these times of suffering, darling
Do you hear me?
O can you see!

I won't fight against my brothers!
I will teach my people to love one another!
I will love my sisters with honor!
I will treat my babe as my only lover!

Because loving, babe, is my way of life!
Because loving, honey, is the way I survive!
Harmony between you and I!
Brings prosperity in this harvest time!

YOU'RE PURE HISTORY FOR EQUALITY

My feelings are deep as the Pacific Ocean!
They're filled with pure love and sincere emotions!
Your beauty is reflected on the sea!
So warm like the water from Acapulco beach!

You are so beautiful and so sweet to me!
Your tenderness restores me completely!
Your breath is so refreshing like the summer breeze!
Cooling me down from my head to my feet!

Your kisses are as sweet as honey!
So tasty and so special like candy!
I love you so much like the whole universe!
I dedicate my rhymes to you on this new verse!

You are the most beautiful flower ever found!
You are the most valuable creation on this ground!
You are so desirable for my eyes to see!
I am able to feel this great fire inside of me!

It's burning me, babe!
It's wishing to have you next to me!
I want to kiss you softly and hold you tight!
I want to get into your mind and reach your heart!

I miss you so bad, and it's so sad!
I wish you were mine, but you're too far!
So we go in life loving each other (my lady)!
Separated by distance from one another, baby!

You are too far but close to me!
You are my roots and my everything!
Your name means lots of things!
You set me free and brought me back complete!

Without you, everything is missing!
With you, my lady, everything is in harmony!
You represent my whole history!
The emancipation of slavery in my country!

Our indigenous people who are still fighting for equality!
The resistance and uprising for dignity!
You taught me to think critically!
You gave me the freedom to set myself free!

You are the beautiful village of the state of my country!
You are pure history for equality!
You are my love
You are my everything

To you I owe this good philosophy
You are the beautiful village of the state of my country
You are pure history for equality

PASSION

ACAPULCO

I am your king,
And you are my queen!
We have a small castle down the beach!
You and I are royalty!

We live in a tropical sea!
A small place but truly happy!
Surrounded by coconut trees!
Mangoes, pineapples, and guava trees!

We wake up with the morning breeze!
Sound of the waves and summer heat!
Singing birds and our community!
Working-class heroes like you and me!

Small houses and lots of kids!
Playing and fishing on the sea!
Singing and chanting in harmony!
Living life as it should be!

Poorly but truly happy!
Working hard for their families!
Loving each other's company!
Small colorful houses in Acapulco Beach!

Surfing and sailing through the sea!
Yachts and cruise ships is all we see!
People from all over the world coming here!
Sailing for pleasure is their final destiny!

Scuba diving, clubbing, and dining is their fantasy!
This is the place to be!
This is the true reason they come here!
Because we live in a tropical sea!

A small place but truly happy!
Surrounded by coconut trees!
Mangoes, pineapples, and guava trees!

We wake up with the morning breeze!
Sound of the waves and summer heat!
Singing birds and our community!
Working-class heroes like you and me!

Small houses and lots of kids!
Playing and fishing on the sea!
Singing and chanting in harmony!
Living life as it should be!

Poorly but truly happy!
Working hard for their families!
Loving each other's company!
Small colorful houses in Acapulco Beach!

Surfing and sailing through the sea!
Yachts and cruise ships is all we see!
People from all over the world coming here!
Sailing for pleasure is their final destiny!

Scuba diving, clubbing, and dining is their fantasy!
This is the place to be!
This is the true reason they come here!
To experience this tropical paradise and its summer heat!

ALL WE NEED IS EACH OTHER

You can be so desirable and so needful
But you can also piss me off!
You can bring me peace and make me feel loved
But you can also break my heart!

You can torture me by ignoring me
But you can also make me fly!
You can make me feel depressed and unwanted
But you can also make me laugh, daydream, and fulfill my entire
life!

Sometimes I hate you
Because I love you so much!
Sometimes I hate myself
Because I'm losing you
And I don't know how to get you back!

I wanna talk to you, but I don't know how to start
'Cause I'm afraid that you might step on me and reject me and
leave my side!
Damn it, sometimes I do wanna cry
Because my heart is in great pain, and I feel like it's the end of
time!

I wanna have you next to me and kiss your sweet mouth!
I wanna tell you that I love you and keep you forever by my side!
I wanna approach you and tell you these words with my own mouth
So you may know the true reason I'm feeling down tonight

'Cause only you can heal this broken heart
With your lovely attention, tenderness, and your understanding, my hidden star!

Girl, if we kick it tonight, we're gonna have so much fun
'Cause we don't need no fancy restaurants and no fancy cars
'Cause all we need tonight is each other under the moonlight and the shiny sky!

Girl, if we kick it every night, we are gonna love each other for life
'Cause all we need every night is some candle lights
Some flowers and a good song
To hold each other, kiss each other, and dance slowly under the moon and the stars
All the way until the morning dawn!

ALLOW ME TO MAKE LOVE TO YOU

If I decide to make love to you, babe
Let it be
Don't stop the moment, darling
It's a natural thing

If you feel my hands caressing your body,
Bear with me
Don't refuse my kisses, little woman
Feel the heat

You are the most beautiful thing
My eyes have ever seen
You are the most desirable pleasure
I have ever lived
Believe in me when I tell you this

Mi Princesita
Todos mis deseos los tengo para ti
Porque tu me enseñaste a vivir
Un mundo nuevo
Lleno de dulsura mi corazón siente por ti
Un amor puro y sincero
Muy dentro de mi

My love for you will always be

Spanish music, romantic phrases, poetry
Dancing, making love to you passionately
While telling you many sweet little things
The moon, the sun, the mountains, and the beach
The fruits, the flowers, your body, and the honey from your lips!

Todo me recuerda a ti
el perfume de tus besos
El sabor de tu dulce aliento
La manera de vivir

I close my eyes, and I can see you here
Very close to me
The sensation of the moment
Holding you tight, babe

Climax
Satisfying all your needs,
Releasing energy to this material world
Pleasant moments full of ecstasy

BOUND TOGETHER

Flowers from the trees are falling!
Tears from your eyes are rolling!

They are falling from the sky, babe
They are rolling from your eyes!
They are falling on the ground, honey
They are watering the plants!

They are fulfilling my thirst, darling
They are conquering my heart!
They are fulfilling this emptiness, babe
They are giving me life!

O yeah, babe
They are giving me life
O yeah, honey
They are reaching my heart!

They are watering my soul, babe
They are fulfilling my heart!
They are watering my spirit, honey
They are giving me life!

O yeah, babe
They are giving me life
O yeah, honey,
They are reaching my heart

They are watering my soul, babe
They are fulfilling my heart!
They are watering my spirit, honey
They are giving me life!

'Cause you and I, darling, are bound!
We are bound, honey
We are bound!

We are bound, babe
We are bound!
We are bound in this beautiful life!

'Cause you know better, babe!
'Cause you know better, honey!
'Cause you know better, darling!
'Cause you are the only one who can make me happy!

You make me feel loved and satisfied!
With your everyday loving and tenderness,
My beautiful sweetheart

CHANGING OUR DESTINY

There is destruction everywhere!
There is corruption in every place!
There is suffering pouring like rain!
There are children, honey, dying today!

Only you and I can see everything!
Only you and I can bring equality!
Only you and I can bring integrity!
Only you and I can change our destiny!

I wanna hold you tight!
I wanna kiss your mouth!
I wanna see your eyes!
I wanna rock your body, babe!
I wanna love you and make you reach the stars!

I'm sitting among the shadows of this chilling night!
I'm looking at the sky, honey
(What a beautiful night!)
The sound of the wind is so precious to me!
The motion on the ocean, darling, satisfies me!

Time goes by so slowly with no worries on my mind!
The weather is so comforting that relaxes my heart!
The waters move so freely across the earth!
The air I breathe brings me tranquility again!

Out of the ashes, this little man will come!
Out of the darkness, this little man will shine!
When you and I, little darling, step out of this world of silence and
try it!

Baby, you smell so nice!
Yeah, darling, you give me butterflies!
Baby, you taste so sweet!
Making love to you, honey, is all I need!

No living thing brings such passion to me!
No living soul can blaze this fire in me!
Don't hate me for being different!
Accept me, baby, for making a difference!

She keeps me amazed, bro
(Like the moon and the stars!)
She looks so beautiful, bro
(Like the palm trees on the ground!)

Love can make you crazy!
Love can make you smile!
Love can make you change!
Love can make you spin around!

Don't brutalize me
(Don't destroy my lasting!)
Don't alienate me
(Don't segregate me!)

My eyes are not crying tonight, Lord!
My feet are rested and warm!
I'm feeling fine looking at the stars, Lord!
I'm lying on a tree having a good quality time!

Lord, please make it last!
Lord, please give me company in this beautiful night!
Because time goes by so slowly with no worries on my mind!
Because the weather is so comforting that relaxes my whole heart!

COME TO ME, BABY

I am afraid of losing you, boo,
Before taking a chance!
I am afraid of confusing you, boo,
Before explaining myself!

I've been waiting for you for so long!
I've been loving you for many moons ago!
I've been calling you in the morning!
I've been calling you when the night falls!

I've been playing for you slow songs!
I've been writing for you romantic poems!
I've been needing your tender sugar!
I've been needing your love!

I've been needing your affection, honey!
I've been needing you while I'm alone!
Because I am so lonely!
Because I am so lost!

So come to me, baby,
And rescue my confused soul!
Beauty comes within ourselves!
True happiness comes by itself!

So don't feel forsaken, little darling!
Don't feel left out, sweet child!
Time will heal the pain from the past!
Time will force you to leave everything behind!

So let's unite and get together tonight!
Let's get together and love each other in life!
'Cause the mood is so sweet!
'Cause the time is so fine!
'Cause my heart desires for your kisses to be mine!

In this time of unification!
In this time of redemption!
In this time of consolation!
In this time of solicitation!

In this sweet and awesome time!
Come to me, baby,
And fulfill this emptiness in my heart!
Come to me, darling,
And become part of this existing life!

Because I've been waiting for you for so long!
I've been loving you for many moons ago!
I've been calling you in the morning!
I've been calling you when the night falls!

I've been playing for you slow songs!
I've been writing for you romantic poems!
I've been needing your tender sugar!
I've been needing your love!

I've been needing your affection, honey!
I've been needing you while I'm alone!

DANCE, BABE

Dance, babe, dance!
Feel free, honey, feel free!
Feel free and laugh!

Sing, babe, sing!
Feel happy, honey, feel happy!
Feel happy and satisfied!

How beautiful it is to laugh!
How peaceful it is to dance!
How sweet is the time!
How pleasant is the moment
(The moment, babe)
The moment when I see you happy and satisfied!

We were born to be free!
We were born to be equal in this beautiful life!

Don't let anyone confuse your heart!
Don't let anyone oppress your beautiful mind!
Don't let anyone track you down!
Don't let anyone make you cry!

Be happy and don't look back!
Be happy, baby
Be happy and enjoy this quality time

Dance, babe, dance!
Feel free, honey, feel free!
Feel free and laugh!

Sing, babe, sing!
Feel happy, honey, feel happy!
Feel happy and satisfied!

Los mares y los rios tienen la misma cosa!
Las aguas de las nuves hacen de esta flor mas hermosa!

Quiero abrasarte poco a poquito!
Quiero gozarme muy despacito!
Quiero hacerte mía en esta noche!
Quiero complacer todos tus deseos nena amorosa!

Dance, babe, dance!
Feel free, honey, feel free!
Feel free and laugh!

Sing, babe, sing!
Feel happy, honey, feel happy!
Feel happy and satisfied!

You blazed all the fire in me, babe,
What can I say!
You blazed all the strong feelings in me
Every day!

Your love is like burning lava, babe
(Your love is like burning lava.)
Burning lava running through the night!

It makes me happy, babe
(It makes me happy.)
It makes me happy and satisfied!

Dance, babe, dance!
Feel free, honey, feel free!
Feel free and laugh!

Sing, babe, sing!
Feel happy, honey, feel happy!
Feel happy and satisfied!

How beautiful it is to laugh!
How peaceful it is to dance!
How sweet is the time!
How pleasant is the moment
(The moment, babe),
The moment when I see you happy and full of life!

Dance, babe, dance!
Feel free, honey, feel free!
Feel free and laugh!

Sing, babe, sing!
Feel happy, honey, feel happy!
Feel happy and satisfied!

How beautiful it is to laugh!
How peaceful it is to dance!
How sweet is the time!
How pleasant is the moment
(The moment, babe),
The moment when I see you happy and full of life!

DEDICATED TO THE ONE I LOVE

The waves are so hard, babe!
The moon is so bright!
The water from the ocean is dancing, honey
(It is dancing!)
It is singing, darling
(It is singing!)
It is singing with me tonight!

The stars on the sky are my companion!
The palm trees and the ocean breeze are cooling me down!
The ocean and my mellow mood—it's all I got!

Rise up from the ocean in the deep blue sky!
Rise up from the waters and sing with me tonight!
Dance into space and travel into time
Dance, baby
Dance, darling, and satisfy my heart!

'Cause I miss you, babe!
I miss you, darling!
I miss your loving and tenderness with me tonight!

The sound of the ocean is so sweet!
The movement of the trees are gentle and brief!
Long hills by the ocean and the refreshing breeze!
Long history for mankind overcoming any grief!
Sweet pearl from the ocean in the winter myth!
Sweet diamonds in the sky shining overseas!

And I'm missing you, babe!
I'm missing you, honey
(I'm missing you here!)

My mind is missing you tonight!
My heart is wishing for you to be mine!
My soul is in love with you
(And here I am alone in the dark!)

Please hear my crying, babe!
Please heal my soul, honey!
Please reach my heart, darling!
Please hear this song and dance with me tonight!

Si pudiera abrasarte estaria muy contento!
Si pudiera besarte te quitaria todo el aliento!
Si pudiera verte hoy todo seria diferente!
Si pudiera tenerte hoy te quedarias en mi mente!

Porque tu amor es tan lindo!
Porque tus labios me seducen cuando estas conmigo!
Porque todo es magnifico en este paraiso!
Porque todo me satisface cuando estoy contigo!

Poetry was given to this simple man!
Poetry was given to express my feelings for her!
Music was given to satisfy my soul!
Music was given to give praises to the one I love!
Dance into space and travel into time
Dance, baby
Dance, darling, and satisfy my heart!

'Cause I miss you, babe!
I miss you, darling!
I miss your loving and tenderness with me tonight!

The sound of the ocean is so sweet!
The movement of the trees are gentle and brief!
Long hills by the ocean and the refreshing breeze!
Long history for mankind overcoming any grief!

DON'T CONFUSE YOUR HEART

I'm gonna love you, babe,
In the good times and the hard times!
I'm gonna take care of you, honey,
In the loveless nights and the weakened times

Never forsake me for a moment
I will always be by your side
You will always be right

No matter what
You will always be mine
In this awesome life

You and I will shine like two bright stars
Up in the sky next to the moon and the sun
Making love with a passionate heart
My soul and mind will be added to your life

Don't let any politics confuse your heart
Love is the key to reunite our loving in these hard times
Angel of mine sent from the highest above
From up in the sky next to the Creator of life

We will survive in this Armageddon
Keep your head up high

I want to hold you tight
So please look into my eyes
I won't make you cry
Love me, babe, like no one else

I want to keep you warm
So please don't say goodbye
Darling, I won't waste your time
Your love is the only thing I got

I want to wrap you into my arms
Kiss you smoothly and softly
For the rest of our lives

How many times will it take you to realize that
Your love is mine?
How many times will it take you to stay with me
And be part of this sweet life of mine?

I love you for what you are
I need you with all my heart
So please, honey, don't confuse your mind
And don't say goodbye

I won't waste your time
Your love is the only thing I got
I want to wrap you into my arms
Kiss you smoothly and softly for the rest of our lives

So please baby hold me tight and stay with me tonight
Please darling be mine and smile to the moonlight
'Cause no matter how hard these times are
You will always be the one I want and my number one

DRIFTING MEMORIES

Your lips were so tasty!
Your kisses were so sweet!
Your cheeks were so soft!

Your face was so beautiful!
Your smile was so meaningful!
Your body was so desirable!

I couldn't wait!
I couldn't, honey!
I couldn't wait to make love to you!

You smiled at me and wished the same!
We started playing games!
So I licked your breast!
I held your hips and kissed your neck!

We were able to fulfill all our fantasies!
In our minds, all we felt was good ecstasy!
Good memories!
Making history!

You moved so high like the high tides!
You moved so low like the low tides!
So fast, so slow!
So nice, so rough!
So passionate and so full of love!

Your lips tasted like tropical fruit!
So desirable, boo!
They got me in the mood!

Making love to you!
Under the stars and a full moon!
Under our roof!
Loving you and pleasing you!

I used to hold your naked body!
Laugh together in the after-party!
Caress your hips! Bite your lips!
While you told me that you love me!

Drifting memories full of ecstasy!
Having fun in our fantasies!

You moved so high like the high tides!
You moved so low like the low tides!
So fast, so slow!
So nice, so rough!
So passionate and so full of love!

Your lips tasted like tropical fruit!
So desirable, boo!
They got me in the mood!

Making love to you!
Under the stars and a full moon!
Under our roof!
Loving you and pleasing you!

I used to hold your naked body!
Laugh together in the after-party!
Caress your hips! Bite your lips!
While you told me that you love me!

Drifting memories full of ecstasy!
Having fun in our fantasies!
Thinking back. Kicking back
Making you laugh

Having fun was the plan
You and I holding us tight
Kissing your mouth. Getting high
Relaxing our minds at all times

I will never forget your lovely face
Your sweet smile was so amazing
You never gave me any stress
But always comprehend that I was the only man

We were so blessed
Until the day I left to another place
The US border was on the way

You couldn't come
I couldn't go
That was the day
Everything came into an end

We can only reminisce the days we spent
Loving us was the way
Many years I have to wait
Becoming legal is the American way

We couldn't wait
I wish you the best
I have to stay
It will be too late

Find another man
That makes you happy
As I used to do it
On those days

ELEVATING MY FEELINGS FOR YOU

You are my reason for living!
You are my queen!
You are my ecstasy!
You are everything to me!

You rock your body
(Like no other!)
You keep me cool
(In a very mellow mood!)

You look so fine
(Like the moon in the sky!)
You please me
And make me feel all right!

Your voice is like a melody!
Your company is so special to me!
Your smile is so comforting!
Your lips are full of loving!

Your absence affects my whole being!
Your fire, baby, burns inside me!
Your tenderness, honey, restores any grief!
Your understanding, darling, is everything to me!
Your loving, girl, restores my whole being!

Elevating my feelings for you is not in vain!
Elevating my love for you is nothing to be ashamed!
Elevating my emotions for you is always gain!
Because your company, little darling, takes away all the pain!

Carita tierna, sonrisa sincera!
Amistad dulce, cuerpo de echisera!
Tu eres muy linda como una estrella!
Tu eres tan hermosa como la luna entera!
Que de todas las mujeres, mi nena
(Tu eres la mas bella!)

Tus labios dulces me dan mucho gozo!
Tu cinturita, mami, me vuelve loco!

Te sientes sola como una rockera!
Y te sientes posada como una cualquiera!
Mas no sabes, mi reina
(Que de todas las mujeres)
Tu eres la mas bella!

Your fire, baby, burns inside me!
Your tenderness, honey, restores any grief!
Your understanding, darling, is everything to me!
Your loving, girl, restores my whole being!

Elevating my feelings for you is not in vain!
Elevating my love for you is nothing to be ashamed!
Elevating my emotions for you is always gain!
Because your company, little darling, takes away all the pain!

Carita tierna, sonrisa sincera!
Amistad dulce, cuerpo de echisera!
Tu eres muy linda como una estrella!
Tu eres tan hermosa como la luna entera!
Que de todas las mujeres, mi nena
(Tu eres la mas bella!)

Tus labios dulces me dan mucho gozo!
Tu cinturita, mami, me vuelve loco!
Te sientes sola como una rockera!
Y te sientes posada como una cualquiera!
Mas no sabes, mi reina
(Que de todas las mujeres)
Tu eres la mas bella!

HOLD ME TIGHT

The moon is in the sky!
The breeze is so sweet!
The ocean and the winds
Are making my soul sing!

How great is the moment, honey
(The moment, baby),
The moment when you are close to me!

You turn on the fire in me,
What can I say!
You blaze all my emotions in me every day!
You make me feel like a real man!

You make me feel so happy
(So happy, darling)
So happy to enjoy this beautiful day!

Your love is so sweet as honey, babe
(So gentle, honey),
So peaceful as the sound of the waves!

It makes me calm down when I get upset!
It makes me want you, darling
(It makes me need you, babe)
It makes me desire you day after day!

I'll be kind to you!
I'll be sweet to you!
I'll be gentle and neat!
I'll be honest and humble, darling!

I'll be the best man that I can be!
I'll be the prince of your dreams, babe!
I'll be a good man when you are close to me!

All you have to do, honey, is just hold me tight!
Hold me stable when I'm falling down
(When I'm falling down, babe),
When I'm falling down in this firepit!

You turn on the fire in me,
What can I say!
You blaze all my emotions in me every day!
You make me feel like a real man!

You make me feel so happy
(So happy, darling),
So happy to enjoy this beautiful day!

Your love is so sweet as honey, babe
(So gentle, honey)
So peaceful as the sound of the waves!

It makes me calm down when I get upset!
It makes me want you, darling
(It makes me need you, babe)
It makes me desire you day after day!

I'll be kind to you!
I'll be sweet to you!
I'll be gentle and neat!
I'll be honest and humble, darling!

I'll be the best man that I can be!
I'll be the prince of your dreams, babe!
I'll be a good man when you are close to me!

All you have to do, honey, is just hold me tight!
Hold me stable when I'm falling down
(When I'm falling down, babe),
When I'm falling down in this firepit!

I DON'T WANT TO SAY GOODBYE

Tell me, why do I miss you so much?
Why do I love to see your classy touch?
Why do I love to see you speak?
Why do I go crazy when I have you with me?

Darling, come and hold me tight
I promise to you I'll treat you right
Honey, come and stay with me
I swear I'll treat you like a lovely queen

Night after night, I dream about you
Time after time, I love you, boo
I want to make love to you
I love you and miss you too

You set me free when I am in need
You get my life complete by being with me
Your voice is like music to my ears
Losing you is what I really fear

I don't want to say goodbye
I want you to forever be mine
You are very important to my life
You are the only one I want

I love the sunlight reflected in your eyes
I need your smile at all times
Your kisses are what I love the most
Your company is what I need at all cost

I'll keep you warm between my arms
Your departure is what my heart alarms
And night after night, I dream about you
And time after time, I love you, boo

You set me free when in need
You get my life complete
By being with me
I don't want to say goodbye

You are very important to my life
You are the only one I want
I love the sunlight reflected in your eyes
I need your smile at all times

Your kisses are what I love the most
Your company is what I need at all cost
I'll keep you warm between my arms
Your departure is what my heart alarms

And I don't want to say goodbye
I don't want to say goodbye, baby
I don't want to say goodbye

I NEED YOUR LOVE BY MY SIDE

I'm lost like an infant
(I'm lost!)
Don't know who my friends are!
I'm lost like an orphan
(I'm lost!)
Don't have any love by my side!

Come to me to comfort me, babe
(Come on!)
Come to hold me tight!
Come to me to groove me, darling
(Come on!)

Come to bring me to paradise!
'Cause I'm lost without you, honey
(I'm lost!)
'Cause I need your love by my side

The sun moves across the heavens
(It moves!)
The wind blows across the earth
(It blows!)

My mind wanders like a spirit in the forest
(It wanders!)
Looking for a peaceful moment to rest!

I cannot hide in the shadows of reality!
I cannot die without living and loving this life!

So let me enjoy this peaceful moment of duality!
Let me bring satisfaction and love to my heart!

'Cause I'm lost without you, honey
(I'm lost!)
'Cause I need your love by my side!
So come to me to comfort me, babe
(Come on!)
Come to hold me tight!
Come to me to groove me, darling
(Come on!)

Come to bring me to paradise!
'Cause I'm lost without you, honey
(I'm lost!)
'Cause I need your love by my side!

The sun moves across the heavens
(It moves!)
The wind blows across the earth
(It blows!)

My mind wanders like a spirit in the forest
(It wanders!)
Looking for a peaceful moment to rest!

I cannot hide in the shadows of reality!
I cannot die without living and loving this life!
So let me enjoy this peaceful moment of duality!
Let me bring satisfaction and love to my heart!

'Cause I'm lost without you, honey
(I'm lost!)
'Cause I need your love by my side!
So come to me to comfort me, babe
(Come on!)
Come to hold me tight!
Come to me to groove me, darling
(Come on!)

Come to bring me to paradise!
'Cause I'm lost without you, honey
(I'm lost!)
'Cause I need your love by my side!

I WANT YOU AND NEED YOU COMPLETELY

I get cold feelings at the nighttime
I have so much pain in my heart
I have too many thoughts on my mind
I have too many tears in my eyes

I miss you so damn much
I love you with all my heart
I'm crying for you tonight
I'm suffering in pain and so sad

I cannot sleep in this cold night
I'm missing you alone in the dark
I'm wanting you and crying aloud
I want to love you like the very first time

You won't find a good lover like me
You won't find another man who sexes you like me
You won't find anyone like me
You won't ever find a man who loves you like me

A man who appreciates your company
A man who understands you completely
A man who is willing to give out everything
A man who won't change your love for anything

Come back to me once again
All this love won't be in vain
Come and heal all this pain
Good feelings is what will remain

Good lovers won't show regret
My heart and mind cannot sustain
Our love and memories were just so great
I just cannot choose another way

It is heaven and hell here
It is so beautiful when you are close to me
It is so painful, all these old memories
It is the choices we make between you and me

Fire is burning inside me
Pain is hurting in here
I cannot get you out of my memories
I cannot let you go without telling you this

I need you more than anything
I want you more than everything
I miss your sweet company
I want you and need you completely

I just cannot choose another way
Our love and memories were just so great
My heart and mind cannot sustain
Good lovers won't show regret

I WILL LOVE YOU

Happiness has come to me again
Hatred has been cast away
Loving and tenderness is what remains
Among this paradise on this living earth

O baby, baby, baby
Brutalize me with your tenderness
Enslave me with your love
On your feet I will surrender

Loving you more and more and more
Segregate me among all men
Marginalize me between your legs
Make love to me like a wild animal
Take good care of me like a living saint

In this confusing world
Heal me from all this pain
Take me to paradise
By carrying my human spirit away

Put your arms around me
Seduce me gently, baby
Give me one night of pleasure, honey
Uplifting me, darling

Emancipate me to a conscious way
I'm just a phone call away
Call me, baby
So I can take all your stress away

I'll be there to save the day
I'll be your hero like superman
I will make you scream my name
Ecstasy in so many ways

I'll be more than just a simple friend
I'll be your lover day after day
I'll make it last

Our love will shine
Two conscious minds
Sharing some quality good time

I won't let you go
I will keep you for the days to come
I will give you true love
I will keep on loving you more and more and more

I'LL BE YOUR FRIEND, LITTLE DARLING

If you need a friend, you can always call on me!
You can always lean on my shoulders, baby!
You can always count on me!

I'll be there in a second, honey!
I'll be there for whatever you need!
I will give you my attention, darling!
If that's what you really need!

I'll be there with you in the hard times!
I'll be there with you in the good times!
I'll be there with you by your side!
I'll be loving you, little darling, until the day we die!

The morning comes, and the night arrives!
And I'm still loving you, baby, with all my heart!
All the good memories, honey!
And all the positive experiences, baby
(Enlightening our lives!)

You are on my mind
(You can't deny!)
We belong to each other in this existing life!
Times are sometimes hard, darling
(But we believe in each other no matter what!)

❦

You trust in me, and I trust in you with my own life!
We'll protect each other as trouble comes!

If you need a friend, you can always call on me!
You can always lean on my shoulders, baby!
You can always count on me!

I'll be there in a second, honey!
I'll be there for whatever you need!

My love for you will always be
(Love and affection in continuous harmony!)
Tranquility among all creations
And duality for all the existing beings!

Feeling sympathy for you and sharing loyalty!
Loving you naturally and unconditionally!
You are on my mind
(You can't deny!)
We belong to each other in this existing life!

Times are sometimes hard, darling
(But we believe in each other no matter what!)
You trust in me, and I trust in you with my own life!
We'll protect each other as trouble comes!

If you need a friend, you can always call on me!
You can always lean on my shoulders, baby!
You can always count on me!

I'll be there in a second, honey!
I'll be there for whatever you need!

My love for you will always be
(Love and affection in continuous harmony!)
Tranquility among all creations and duality for all the existing
beings!
Feeling sympathy for you and sharing loyalty!
Loving you naturally and unconditionally!

I'M ALL ALONE, BABE

The night is falling, babe!
My dreams are growing!
My wishes and desires to see you, girl, are greater than the
beautiful sun!
My heart misses you like the moon and the stars!
My soul desires you, darling, like the springs of living water up in
the sky!

But here I am lonely with a broken heart!
Here I am, babe, missing you continuously and so bad!
The night is so lonely, and the weather is so cold!
The grass is so green, it makes my heart rejoice!
The thought about you, girl, makes my tears fall!

And I'm alone!
I'm alone, babe!
I'm alone in this mellow mood reasoning and stoned!

I'm alone!
I'm alone, honey!
I'm alone trying to set myself free in a cloud of smoke!

I'm alone, darling!
I'm alone!
I'm alone trying to heal myself with positive thoughts!

I wish I could be able to fly!
I wish I could be able to reach the sky!
I wish I could be able to reach your heart!

But I'm alone!
I'm alone, babe!
I'm alone in this mellow mood reasoning and stoned!

I'm alone!
I'm alone, honey!
I'm alone trying to set myself free in a cloud of smoke!

I'm alone, darling!
I'm alone!
I'm alone trying to heal myself with positive thoughts!

The night is so lonely, and the weather is so cold!
The grass is so green, it makes my heart rejoice!
The thought about you, girl, makes my tears fall!

And I'm alone!
I'm alone, babe!
I'm alone in this mellow mood reasoning and stoned!

I'm alone!
I'm alone, honey!
I'm alone trying to set myself free in a cloud of smoke!

I'm alone, darling!
I'm alone!
I'm alone trying to heal myself with positive thoughts!

I wish I could be able to fly!
I wish I could be able to reach the sky!
I wish I could be able to reach your heart!

But I'm alone!
I'm alone, babe!
I'm alone in this mellow-mood reasoning and stoned!

I'm alone!
I'm alone, honey!
I'm alone trying to set myself free in a cloud of smoke!

I'm alone, darling!
I'm alone!
I'm alone trying to heal myself with positive thoughts!

I'm alone trying to think about new ways to approach you, girl!
I'm alone trying to find new ways to make us fall in love!
I'm alone trying to write about these feelings in this new poem!

IF I HAD A CHANCE TO BE WITH YOU

This love and desire to see you
Have given me the hope to fulfill this very special need!
I breathe sexual fantasies in my memory,
And my heart beats in a special melody!

If I had a chance to be with you,
It would fulfill my most intimate fantasy!
I would travel through your whole body inch by inch!
Exploring your naked body from your head to your feet!

I would take my time contemplating the beauty between your hips!
I would hold your breast and lick your neck!
I would make you scream of pleasure and ecstasy!
I would make you see all the beauty within my soul!

I would help you reach your most intimate fantasies!
I would stay with you for as long as I could!
I would be showing affection, my darling, sincerely and
continuously!
I would remain faithful to you, my love, forever and
unconditionally!

I would be loving you madly in this life and for eternity!
I would be spending my time wisely with your company!
I would be smiling and screaming that I have you next to me!
I would be loving you unconditionally and for eternity!

I'M DR. LOVE (PERFORMING AFFECTION)

I want to sing for you, babe, a sweet song like a grown-up cicada!
I want to express all my emotions, honey, in a perfect song that I
just made up!
I want to use some of the most sexual and descriptive rhymes!
I want to hit just the perfect spot right in your heart!

I want to sexually attract you and just make you mine!
I want to hold you tight and kiss your sweet mouth!
I want to lick your breast and bite your neck tonight!
I want to smell your hair and love you softly, darling, night after
night!

I want to make you sweat
I want to make you mine!
I want to satisfy all your most intimate desires in this lovely night!
I'm going to push it hard!

I'm going to reach your climax, babe, time after time!
I'm going to love you right!
I'm going to sexually love you, honey,
With all the passion held inside!

Tonight is the perfect night!
Tonight I'm going to love you roughly, darling,
Under the stars and the moonlight!
That's right, I'm going to reach satisfaction with the injection
tonight!

Action, I'm Dr. Love performing affection on bed (all night)!
Perfection, that's the intention of the game we are playing tonight!
Loving you madly is the act of creation that is keeping us alive!
You can't deny you feel the same sexual desires for both of us!

The moon is so bright, and the stars are shining in the sky!
Our bodies are completely wet, and our minds are hypnotized!
You keep on calling me, baby, and I keep on making you mine!
I'm leaving my marks all over your body as you hold me tight!

Work it, babe, come on!
I'm Dr. Love performing affection on bed all night!
Perfection, that's the intention of the game we are playing tonight!
You can't deny you feel the same sexual desires for both of us!

The moon is so bright,
And the stars are shining in the sky!
Our bodies are completely wet,
And our minds are hypnotized!

You keep on calling me, baby,
And I keep on making you mine!
I'm leaving my marks all over your body
As you hold me tight!

Work it, babe, come on!
I'm Dr. Love performing affection on bed (all night)!
Perfection, that's the intention of the game we are playing tonight!
Loving you madly is the act of creation that's keeping us alive!

IT'S RAINING AND POURING IN TEARS

It's raining so hard, darling!
It's pouring so bad!
I wish I can stop the rain, babe!
I wish I can stop the time!

'Cause I'm falling, honey!
I'm falling (and falling) and falling so hard!

I need someone to lift me up!
I need someone to hold me tight!
I need someone to give me company!
I need someone to hear me cry!

'Cause it's raining (it's raining), it's raining tonight!
'Cause I'm shaking (I'm shaking), I'm shaking so bad!
So please hear the cry (the cry), the cry of my heart!
'Cause I need some shelter and love by my side

The water is falling (and falling) and falling so hard!
The rain is pouring (and pouring) and pouring in tears from my eyes!
I feel so lonely, disappointed, and sad!
I feel so cold, shaky, and mad!

‘Cause it’s raining (it’s raining), it’s raining tonight!
‘Cause I’m shaking (I’m shaking), I’m shaking so bad!
So please hear the cry (the cry), the cry of my heart!
‘Cause I need some shelter and love by my side!

The water keeps on falling (and falling) and falling so hard!
The rain keeps on pouring (and pouring) and pouring in tears from
my eyes!
I feel so lonely, disappointed, and sad!
I feel so cold, shaky, and mad!

‘Cause it’s raining (it’s raining), it’s raining tonight!
‘Cause I’m shaking (I’m shaking), I’m shaking so bad!
So please hear the cry (the cry), the cry of my heart!
‘Cause I need some shelter and love by my side!”

It’s raining so hard, darling!
It’s pouring so bad!
I wish I can stop the rain, babe!
I wish I can stop the time!

‘Cause I’m falling, honey!
I’m falling (and falling) and falling so hard!

LOVEMAKING

All I wanna do
Is get lost with you!
All I wanna have
Is your body next to mine!

Get lost in this love
Get lost in your arms!
Get lost in this fantasy
Get lost with you tonight!

Oh, up and down
(Up and down)
To the sides!

Oh, up and down
(Up and down)
Is so nice!

You move like the ocean in the high tides
You move like the winds so gentle tonight
Don't stop!
Keep on moving freely to the sky!
Don't stop!
Make me happy every night!

My heart is with you
Until the morning dawn!
My life is for you
Now and in the future to come!

O, que bonito!
(Que bonito)
Que bonito
(Es tu cuerpo al amar)

Que bonito es tu pelo!
(Que bonito, mi nena)
Que bonito es tu pelo
(En el alta mar)

I'm making you sweat,
So hold me tight!
Receive of my love, babe,
And be satisfied!

Don't you love my loving, darling?
Don't you love my presence, honey?
So if you do!
Then hold me tight!

And close your eyes
(Close your eyes, babe!)
And enjoy of my loving
In this beautiful trance!

I don't wanna stop loving you tonight!
I don't wanna stop making love to you!
I don't wanna stop holding you tight!
I don't wanna stop holding you, darling!
I don't wanna stop holding you, honey!
I don't wanna stop moving inside!

Do you love my loving?
Do you want me inside?
Do you feel the chills?
Do you like this quality time?
Do you want to keep on loving each other?

So close your eyes!
Love me like no one else
(Love me, darling)
Love me until the morning comes!

LET OUR LOVE LEAD THE WAY

I am a human being, babe!
I am a very special seed!
I am someone who loves life, honey!
I am someone who appreciates freedom within!

Please take care of me, darling
(Take care of me, honey!)
Take good care of me continuously!

'Cause I am thirsty, babe!
'Cause I am hungry, darling!
'Cause I need your love and affection with me!

Ever since I laid my eyes on you, girl,
My heart skipped a beat!
Ever since I saw you, boo,
My soul rejoiced in a symphony!

And there you are crying again
Oh no!
There you are lost and confused!

It's not easy to talk about feelings, you know!
It's not easy to deny my feelings for you!
I know you want to see me today!
As I want to see you again!

I know you want to hear what I say!
I know you want to lie on my bed!
I know you want to heal your distress!

So come to me, babe, and let's make love on this sunset!
Let this love be the way!
Let all our emotions lead the way!
Let our love forever be there!
Let our fantasies heal this distress!

'Cause the moon is already there!
'Cause the fire is already blazed!
'Cause my bed is already set!
'Cause my door is already open for you, babe!

So let's get together and heal this distress!
Please take care of me, darling!
Take good care of me continuously!

'Cause I am thirsty, babe!
'Cause I am hungry, darling!
'Cause I need your love and affection with me today!
'Cause every time I laid my eyes on you, girl, my heart skipped a beat!

Ever since I saw you, boo,
My soul is rejoiced in a symphony!

But there you are crying again
Oh no!
There you are lost and confused!

It's not easy to talk about feelings, you know!
It's not easy to deny my feelings for you!
I know you want to see me today!
As I want to see you again!

I know you want to hear what I say!
I know you want to lie on my bed!
I know you want to heal your distress!

So come to me, babe, and let's make love on this sunset!
Let this love be the way!
Let all our emotions lead the way!
Let our love forever be there!
Let our fantasies heal this distress!

'Cause the moon is already there!
'Cause the fire is already blazed!
'Cause my bed is already set!
'Cause my door is already open for you, babe!

So let's get together and heal this distress!

LET OUR LOVE RISE

Everything is way more beautiful when you are next to me!
Time goes by so smooth with the ocean breeze!

The sun shines so bright in the sky!
The moon and the stars light up our path!
The movement of the ocean never stops!
The wind embraces us as the days go by!

We sing and dance!
We love each other as the night arrives!
We make passionate love, babe!
We make passionate love until the next sunrise!

Girl, you're on my mind so close to my heart!
Love me as I love you with great remarks!

Would you please be mine?
Let's love each other under the moon and the stars!
Bring me to paradise!

We've finally found true love in this lifetime!
Let our love rise!
Let it shine in the hard times!
Let it be there when you want to lift yourself up!

Everything is way more beautiful when you are next to me!
Time goes by so smooth with the ocean breeze!

The sun shines so bright in the sky!
The moon and the stars light up our path!
The movement of the ocean never stops!
The wind embraces us as the days go by!

We sing and dance!
We love each other as the night arrives!
We make passionate love, babe!
We make passionate love until the next sunrise!

Girl, you're on my mind so close to my heart!
Love me as I love you with great remarks!

Would you please be mine?
Let's love each other under the moon and the stars!
Bring me to paradise!

We've finally found true love in this lifetime!
Let our love rise!
Let it shine in the hard times!
Let it be there when you want to lift yourself up!

LET'S BE TOGETHER, BABE

You will never find love like the one I feel inside
Deep in my heart, true love increasingly lies
Your sweet love is mine, the feeling is so right
Let me love you for the rest of my life

The first time on our first night
Let's make passionate love until the next sunlight
Don't ever cry, wipe the tears from your eyes
Love me unconditionally as I love you deep inside

Smile for me, sweetheart, I will always treat you right
You're very lovely and my love at first sight
Wipe the tears on your eyes
Don't ever cry
Smile, and everything is going to be all right

I miss you so bad
I want you by my side
I wanna love you for the rest of my life
I close my eyes, and I can still see you inside

You're in my mind worshiped as the Most High
You're like the moon deep in the sky
You're like a star shining so bright
You're like the sun giving me light

You're like the water giving me life
You're like the air keeping me alive
So I tell you with all my heart,
I love you, babe,

Let's make love tonight
Let's waste no time
Let's do it
Let's enter into paradise

Let's love each other for life
Let's live together as one
Let's lift each other up high
Let's be together, darling
Let's stick together until the end of time

LET'S KEEP ON DANCING

My heart is broken in two
My tears are falling down too
My life is divided for sure
My spirit wants to be united, boo

Too much confusion among mankind
Too much division has broken my heart
Too many hatreds I see upon my path
Too many rejections I get all the time

But I will survive, honey
I will survive
I will survive, darling
I will survive

I will survive to see unification upon mankind
So let's keep on dancing tonight
Let's keep on crying to the Most High
Let's keep on walking through the dark side
Let's keep on loving each other, babe—until the morning comes

Follow the music, honey
Follow the drumbeat
Follow this music, darling
Follow it with me

Follow the music, babe
Follow it, my dear
Follow the music, sweetie
'Cause it is so special to me

Oh, how beautiful it is, babe
How beautiful you are to me
How beautiful the music is
How special is the feeling within

Let's keep on dancing, babe
Let's keep on following the drumbeat
Let's keep on loving each other, honey
Let's keep on trying to create something here

Let's keep on holding each other, darling
O yeah—until you give yourself a chance to be with me

LET'S WALK TOGETHER

Babe, I love your physical attraction
Honey, you bring great satisfaction
Your love means everything to me
Your tenderness brings good energy

Don't ever leave my side
I don't want ever to say goodbye
I want for both of us to fall in love
I need for both of us to take control

Darling, I need you in my life
Would you please be my wife?
Please walk next to me
Hold my hand and stay with me

Be my special friend
Never again leave this place
I'm telling you from the start
Please be my wife

You're always on my mind
Next to my heart
You put a spell on me
Girl, I need you with me

You take my breath away
Please I want you to stay
Be my wife in this paradise
Stay with me for a lifetime

From all the flowers
In this special garden,
I'm picking you
Don't wanna change my point of view

You're the one I choose
To be my boo
Let's be together
Always and forever

In the hard times
And the good times
Upon this earth,
I will forever be there

While I live,
I won't ever leave
Please hold my hand
I'll be your man

You'll be my woman
I'll be a good man
Under the cold and the rain
There shall be no pain

I'll keep you warm
I'll be your sun
You'll be my start
In this paradise

Under my roof,
I'll provide shelter and food
You'll provide your attention
No lamentations

No regrets
Only success
Positivity
No negativity

You will be my queen
I'll be your king
I will love you madly
I will treat you kindly

Hold my hand and walk next to me
Be my special friend and take good care of me
I'll be your man
You'll be my woman

Let's walk together
Always and forever
In this lifetime
Until death do us part

LIVING IN HARMONY IN OUR OWN REALITY

Here we go in this same road, my sweet love!
Feeling this human desire to love you now and forevermore!
Heal me and restore me with unconditional love!
Embrace me and love me plenty enough!

There hasn't been anyone in this life sweet enough!
No one like you who truly loves me madly enough!
No one whom I can say this is true love!

Your love is more precious than silver, money, and gold!
Your love is the ultimate feeling ever felt!
It's the perfect stage of being on this earth!
You are playful, emotional, and sweet enough!

You are so special to me, and I cannot lie!
You stole my heart and enlighten my mind!
You are the perfect woman for me,
And I need you in my life!

There are no words that could explain
These crazy feelings felt for you!
There is no woman more special than you, girl!

You are my boo,
And all my desires are for you!
You are my queen,
And I am your king!

We are both royalty, and there is loyalty between you and me!
There is no difference in social class or hierarchy!
There are no servants because we are both equal!
There is no war or battles to fight because there is only peace!

We live in harmony and continuous ecstasy!
We live happily and originally!
You and me for eternity in our own reality!

LOVE

Love is the key to unified humanity in this society
Love is to me the most precious thing
Love is to be kind and compassionate
towards animals, plants and human beings

Love is the ultimate feeling!
The desire to see you!
The temptation of kissing you!
The pleasure of having you!

It's to caress your lovely face!
Hold your hips, bite your neck!
Make sweet love to you!
All night and day until the next sunset!
Until we run out of breath!
Until we're ready again!

Love is the willingness to make it work!
Mutual support, unconditional love!
Understanding and bringing hope!
And lots of joy for all lovebirds!

True love is more precious than gold!
More meaningful than a love song!
The opposite of war!
The inspirational note of this sweet poem!

Love is to forgive and redeem past deeds!
It is to bloom in this society!
It is to grow as humanity!
It is to make people see true potential in you and me!
It is to focus on improving our own destiny!
It is to be thankful for the good things we see!

Love is kissing you all over
Making you scream of passion
Making you confirm that this is the true reason
To live for and to fight for!

Love is the key to unified humanity!
It is the missing link that everyone needs
To forgive and improve this society!

Therefore, I surrender
On my knees to love,
For it is the reason that my heart
Still beats and remains in control

LOVE ME LIKE NO ONE ELSE

Days had passed,
And I haven't seen your lovely face
Feelings about you are really hard to contend
I miss you every single day

I want to see you again
My love for you is increasing every moment that it can
I will see you again
In my dreams, you will always be there

'Cause I love you
In a very special way
'Cause I adore you
More than I love my own self

That is why, my love, I am telling you always
Keep this no longer a secret in your head
Because it contains my true feelings
For a very pretty lady like your own self

I wanna love you, baby, like I love water and the air
I want to need you, honey, like living oxygen to my breath
I want to touch you, darling, in a very special way
I want to embrace you, sweety, like my only love on this earth

I want to be together with you in every single moment that I can
All you have to do, baby, is just love me in the same way,
Love me like no one else,
And be together with me, my darling, day after day

You are the star that shines up there in the sky
You are the light that gives love to my heart
You are the ocean wave that carries the sunlight
You are the hope given to me that's keeping me alive

I love you more than anything in this life
I need you more than everything to survive
I want to love you like in the very first time
I want to have you for the rest of my life

'Cause you are the love of my life
'Cause you are so essential to my lifetime

I need you, darling,
Like water and oxygen
At a daily basis time after time

LOVING IS THE WAY I SURVIVE

I'm gonna give you some sweet love, baby
I'm gonna rock your world
I'm gonna show you love and affection, honey
I'm gonna bring some tenderness for both of us

None of us need to feel lonely, darling
None of us need to cry
None of us need to suffer, honey
None of us need to feel so sad

The more we love each other
The more we gain the fight
The more we get close to each other
The more we fulfill this happy life

So here we go on this precious road
Here we go with happiness in our soul

We can talk about love, my darling
We can talk about both of us
We can talk about our feelings, honey
We can talk about them all you want

The time has come for us not to fight
The time has come for our love to survive

From the earth to the sky
From the sky to the sun
From the sun to the whole universe
Our sweet love will forever be bright

It will overcome any sad moments, sweet darling
It will bring us laughter time after time
Thinking about a better future for both of us
Thinking about us, honey, as the days go by

Giving thanks to Mother Earth
Giving thanks to the Most High
It is the righteous path, my darling
It is the way we survive

It is this intimate relationship
Between the creation and the Most High

Praises be to the Father of Creation
Praises be to the only one
From our soul to His heart
From our mouth to His eyes

Human race will unite
Together we'll sing new psalms
Together, baby,
We'll give new praises to the Most High

LOVING THIS GAME

I could make love to you now
And try to work it out tomorrow
Or I could try to work it out now
And make love to you tomorrow

Either way, I still get to make love to you
No matter what decision we make, whatever it takes
I still get to lie down with you on my bed
I still get to contemplate your naked body in my own way

From the rising sun to the sunset
From the falling night to a brand-new day
Playing sexual games
Making love to you softly with no distress

You are my getaway to a perfect place
The perfect stage of reality on earth

Loving ourselves with passion
Releasing stress every single minute we spend
Catching our breath
Sweating ourselves
Kissing each other like crazy every single second that we can

                          —⟨ɔ/ɔ/ɔ⟩—

This is how we spend quality time between ourselves

No excuses, no regrets
No worries and no concerns

Living the moment while we can
Enjoying ourselves
Loving ourselves
Reaching our climax as many as we can

Pulling your hair
Biting your neck
Licking your breast
Holding your legs
Screaming my name

Feeling good about ourselves
Loving this game
As much as we can

MAKING LOVE

Love of mine
You and I
Reaching the sky
Making love in this passionate night

Touching the stars
Contemplating the sun
Kissing your lips
While looking into your eyes

Embracing your heart
Moving like the ocean
In the high and low tides
Going rough
Going soft
Going into your mind
Fulfilling my life with pleasure night after night

You're so wonderful to my eyes
So special like the beautiful sunlight

You are the reason for this happiness
You are all my life
You are so beautiful
You are so fine

You make me daydream and even fly
You make me desire you in the cool nights,
So never mind

Let's make love to one another
Throughout the stages of life
Let's enjoy one another
Under the moon, the sun, and the stars

O love of mine
You and I
Reaching the sky
Making love in this passionate night

Touching the stars
Contemplating the sun
Kissing your lips
While looking into your eyes

Embracing your heart
Moving like the ocean
In the high and low tides
Going rough
Going soft
Going into your mind
Fulfilling my life with pleasure night after night

You're so wonderful to my eyes
So special like the beautiful sunlight

You are the reason for this happiness
You are all my life
You are so beautiful
You are so fine

You make me daydream and even fly
You make me desire you in the cool nights,
So never mind

Let's make love to one another
Throughout the stages of life
Let's enjoy of one another
Under the moon, the sun, and the stars

MAKING LOVE IS OUR MAIN OBJECTIVE

O babe,
Babe, you smell so good
Your female essence smells like perfume

O darling,
Darling, your lips are so sweet
Your beauty gets stuck in my memory

I close my eyes,
And I am able see you in there
I hold you tight,
And I feel so blessed

I feel so happy all over my face
All over my body,
I feel extremely content

I believe you're the one for me, honey
I can see it in our eyes, baby
You make my life complete

O darling,
Darling, I love you so madly
I can see it in your lips

How sweet is loving you, honey
Licking you from your head to your feet
You're my inspiration, sugar

Contemplating all your beauty is my occupation
Don't lose my concentration, honey
Your beauty, baby, is of great admiration

I'm not going to waste my time
Making love to you in the middle of the night
I'm not going to make you cry
I'm going to make you smile after I make you mine

And here we go in the morning dawn
Still making love to you in the rising sun
Your nakedness is my paradise

Making love to you, baby,
It feels so fine
Ride on me, my darling,
For as long as you want
Bite me gently, honey,
Time after time

The sun is shining so bright
The air is so refreshing for both of us
Your lips are so tight
Makes me want to love you, baby,
At all times

So here we are together in this awesome act
Experiencing pure pleasure, darling, loving us
Here we are going through some ecstasy
Fulfilling all our fantasies happily ever after, darling

Living in the same reality, honey
Together for once you and me
With the same dream
And the same human needs

Making love is our main objective
So gently and sometimes so desperate
Here we are loving us, baby
So gently and sometimes so roughly
So madly, darling, so unconditional
So unforgettable, honey, and so very comfortable

MAKING LOVE WITH PASSION AND LUST

I'm going to give you kisses in the morning
I'm going to make love to you at night
I'm going to whisper that I love you
I'm going to bring you flowers from time to time

I'm going to be there when you need me
I'm going to be there when you cry
I'm going to tell you that you're beautiful, baby
I'm going to wipe the tears from your eyes

I'm going to make you laugh
I'm going to love you my entire life
In these cold nights, I'm going to hold you tight
I'm going to scream to the heavens above that I need you as my
wife

I'm going to hold your hand
I'm going to be more than just a friend
I'm going to be there with you until the end
I wanna be your only man

Listen and observe
This is not a test
Ask yourself if you really love me
And if you will always be there

Let true love lead the way
Let my love for you never be in vain
Let it manifest itself
Let our intentions never fail

Let our emotions prevail
If I really love you
And you really love me
Let us be together

Let me kiss you all over, baby
Let me lick you all over, honey
Until you tell me to stop
All we want, little darling, is to have a pretty good time

Having fun under the moon and the stars
Having a blast until the next sunlight
Making love with passion and lust
Satisfying all our needs and wants

MELLOW MOOD

O time will come
O time will go

My life is hard
My mood is low
I feel so sad
Your love is gone

I miss you
I miss you, darling
I miss you
I miss you even more

O sweet living morning
O sweet living night
O sweet living kisses
O sweet living life
My love is gone from my side

My babe
My love
My darling
O my lady
—has broken my heart

I miss you
I miss you, darling
I miss you
O I miss you even more

I woke up, and you were gone
I got up and lost control
Babe, I'm dying alone
O babe, babe, babe, I miss you even more

I'm hoping to see you tonight
I'm missing you alone in the dark
I'm dreaming about you by my side
I'm waiting and waiting
—And waiting
And waiting for you to arrive

O sweet living morning
O sweet living night
O sweet living kisses
O sweet living life
My love is gone from my side

My babe
My love
My darling
O my lady
—has already broken my heart

I miss you
I miss you, darling
I miss you
O I miss you even more

I miss you in this lonely morning.
I miss you in this lonely night.
I miss you in this mellow mood.
I miss you more in this darkened path.

I miss you
I miss you, darling
I miss you
O I miss you even more

I miss you in this lonely morning.
I miss you in this lonely night.
I miss you in this mellow mood.
I miss you more in this darkened path.

I'm hoping to see you tonight
I'm missing you alone in the dark
I'm dreaming about you by my side
I'm waiting and waiting
—And waiting
And waiting for you to arrive

I miss you
I miss you, darling
I miss you
O I miss you even more

I miss you in this lonely morning.
I miss you in this lonely night.
I miss you in this mellow mood.
I miss you more in this darkened path.

MISSING YOU

O time will come,
O time will go!
My life is hard,
My mood is low!

I feel so sad,
Your love is gone!
My babe, my love!
My darling is gone!

My everything in this world
My beautiful girl
My beautiful star!
My beautiful sunshine!

Music is playing so sad!
Pain is coming from my heart!
Tears are falling down my eyes!
My emotions, honey (my emotions)!
My emotions are driving me mad!

I miss you,
I miss you, honey!
I miss you
I miss you so badly tonight!

I woke up, and you were gone!
I think of you and lose control!
I tried to find you!
And you were gone!

I'm hoping to see you tonight!
I'm missing you alone at the house
I miss your kisses (I miss your company)!
I'm waiting and waiting for you to arrive!

Tears are falling down my eyes!
Tears are falling down my eyes, babe!
Tears are falling down my eyes!

I miss you, honey (I miss you)
I miss you, babe (I miss you)
I miss you alone at the house

My emotions, babe!
My emotions, darling!
My emotions
Are driving me mad!

Music is playing so sad!
Pain is coming from my heart!
Tears are falling down my eyes!
Tears are falling down my eyes, babe!
Tears are falling down tonight!

My emotions
My emotions, darling!
My emotions
My emotions are driving me mad!

I miss you, honey (I miss you)
I miss you, babe (I miss you)
I miss you alone at the house

I miss you, honey
I miss you
I miss you, darling,
I miss you
I miss you so bad
Yeah...

MISSING YOU ALONE IN THE DARK

The moon is in the sky
The stars are so bright
My mind is thinking about you, baby
My heart is missing you in this cold night

Tears are falling down my eyes, honey
I'm missing you alone in the dark
I'm missing your body, darling,
As I close my eyes

I can see your sweet mouth
I can contemplate your lovely smile
And I'm missing you like crazy tonight
You're so beautiful and so smart

You're so understanding
About what I go through in life
With you, everything is so peaceful and so fine
Without you, everything pisses me off

Holidays are coming up
And I'm missing you like crazy tonight
Tears are falling down my eyes
They're falling
They're rolling as many as the stars on the dark gray sky

I'm missing you, mama
I'm wanting you more than my own life

Slow music is playing so loud
Smoke is coming from my mouth
Empty beers are rolling on the ground
And I'm missing you, darling

I'm missing you so much
As I get drunk and high
I can't deny
It's healing the pain from deep inside

I'm missing you like crazy in this cold night
I wish I could hold you tight
Make passionate love under the moonlight

'Cause you are the only one I need and want
'Cause I'm missing you alone in the dark
'Cause I'm missing you like crazy in this cold night

Tears are falling down my eyes
Tears are rolling down tonight
And I'm missing you like crazy in this cold night

Tears are falling down my eyes, baby
They're falling down
They're rolling as many as the stars in the dark gray sky

I'm missing you, mama
I'm wanting you more than my own life

MISSING YOU BY THE OCEAN

It's a beautiful and relaxing day, my friends!
It's a beautiful morning with the sound of the waves!
The breeze is so sweet and refreshing upon my face!
The sun is shining so cool with some flying birds!

I miss you, babe
(I miss you even more today!)
I miss you more in these winter days!
I miss you in this lonely morning more than yesterday!

'Cause you bring great happiness and a big smile on my face!
'Cause your love is sweeter than a sugarcane!

I miss you on these winter days!
I miss you in this lonely morning more than yesterday!

Life is meant to be enjoyed with great inner peace in our soul!
Life is meant to be freed from corruption and be replaced with
pure love!
Life is meant to bring us understanding and love for the poor!

But for some reason, people don't let go of their evil ways!
People don't let go of their genocide consents!
They use me whenever they need support!
And they get rid of me whenever they don't need me anymore!

So here I am, babe!
Here I am by the ocean contemplating the waves!
Here I am relaxing in my mellow mood with the flying birds!
Here I am, babe!
Here I am meditating and missing you today!

I miss you, babe!
I miss you more in these winter days!
Your beautiful face is running all around inside my head!
I miss you in this lonely morning more than yesterday!

'Cause you bring great happiness and a big smile on my face!
'Cause your love is sweeter than a sugarcane!

I miss you on these winter days!
I miss you in this lonely morning more than yesterday!

Life is meant to be enjoyed with great inner peace in our soul!
Life is meant to be freed from corruption and be replaced with
pure love!
Life is meant to bring us understanding and love for the poor!

But for some reason, people don't let go of their evil ways!
People don't let go of their genocide consents!
They use me whenever they need support!
And they get rid of me whenever they don't need me anymore!

So here I am, babe!
Here I am by the ocean contemplating the waves!
Here I am relaxing in my mellow mood with the flying birds!
Here I am, babe!
Here I am meditating and missing you today!

MOVING ACROSS THE OCEAN

The sky is so blue, babe!
The ocean is so cool!
The isolation in me, honey,
Makes me want you!

Lying down next to you
(Lying down, darling)
Lying down in a mellow mood!

The waves are moving next to you
(They are moving, babe)
They are moving along with you!

My hands are caressing you, boo
Very nicely, very gently, darling
Like the sun on the ocean making love too!
Grooving next to you, honey!

Moving inside you!
Moving into your sea, darling
(Moving in you)
Moving across the ocean, babe
Moving along with you!

We go hard, darling,
We go slow!
We go deep, sweet honey,
We go low!

We move across the ocean, honey!
We are moving
(We are moving)

Do you feel it?
O I like it
(I like it, babe)
I like it even more

Lying down next to you
(Lying down, darling)
Lying down in a mellow mood!

The waves are moving next to you
(They are moving, babe)
They are moving along with you!

My hands are caressing you, boo
Very nicely, very gently, darling
Like the sun on the ocean making love too!
Grooving next to you, honey!

Moving inside you!
Moving into your sea, darling
(Moving in you)
Moving across the ocean, babe
Moving along with you!

We go hard, darling,
We go slow!
We go deep, sweet honey,
We go low!

We move across the ocean, honey!
We are moving
(We are moving)

Do you feel it?
O I like it
(I like it, babe)
I like it even more

We go hard, darling,
We go slow!
We go deep, sweet honey,
We go low!

We move across the ocean, honey!
We are moving
(We are moving)

Do you feel it?
O I like it
(I like it, babe)
I like it even more

MY LOVE INCREASES FOR YOU

I wish I was your eyes
So I could see myself through them
So I could see myself the way you see me
And understand the things you like,
The things you love,
The things you hate,
And the things that drive you mad about me

I wish I could be your hair
So I could caress your lovely face
And be able to comprehend the beauty
Found on each part of your face

I wish I could be your lips
So I could kiss them from deep within,
Be able to understand the voices that speak through them
When kindness is used to describe good things

I wish I was able to be your heart
So I could give myself some extra love
With lots of hope
That will unite us more while maintaining self-control

I wish I was able to know your thoughts
So I could be able to know
What you are thinking about me
When I am not close to you

I wish I was able to read your mind
Because, baby, you are my only one
In this wonderful world of pleasure

Because, honey, I miss you
As the sun misses the summer
And the winter misses the snow

I miss you like the bees miss the honey
And the honey misses a rose
I miss you more than the hours miss the day
And the days miss the month
And the month misses the year

I miss you more than yesterday
Because today I miss you more than ever
Never assume I have forgotten about you
Because I breathe for you,
I live for you,
I bow to you in every single moment that I can

In reality, you are out there,
Perhaps not even thinking about me,
But I do think about you more than I think about myself

Because I see your face every single second of every moment that I
can,
And because of it, my love for you increases very strong and super
intense.

NEW OPPORTUNITY

Your lips are so sweet!
Your voice is so nice!
My heart desires you!
My body wants to make you mine!

I wanna hold you tight!
I wanna see your eyes!
While I'm loving you!

I wanna make you mine!
I wanna make you scream!
I wanna reach your heart!

Full of passion, babe!
I wanna make you whine!
There is no time to waste!

We gotta reach the sky!
We gotta love each other!
We gotta remain playful tonight!

The time goes by so smooth!
The moon is so bright!
Your face looks so beautiful!
Your smile looks so nice!

Do you love me, babe?
Do you love me not?
Should I stay with you?
Should I leave you behind?

I am in love with you!
I can't ever leave your side!
I can't ever hate you!
I can't ever make you cry!

Love can make you crazy!
Love can make you smile!
Love can make you hate me!
Love can make you want me!
Love can make you put your feet on the ground!

And I see the rising sun on your lovely eyes!
I see a new opportunity for our love to last!
I see our own generation moving forward hand by hand!
I see a brand-new future for all of us!

We have defeated stereotypes!
We have overcome indigenous people's genocide!
We have rewritten our history left behind!
We have reached full equality for all mankind!

O SWEET LOVE

Give me one more night
(O sweet love!)
Give me one more chance
(I'll treat you right!)

Give me one opportunity
(I will never make you cry!)
Give me all your life
(I'll give you mine!)

Let's love each other like no one else!
Let's keep it tender and alive!
Let's keep it glowing in the dark!
Let's keep on loving each other for life!

O sweet love!
O child of mine!
Smile with the rising sun!
Wipe your tears from your eyes!

Start loving me,
And let's make it last!
Let it all pass!
Leave everything behind!

Let's start from scratch!
Let us rise up
(Keep on loving me!)
And let's love each other for a lifetime!

O sweet love!
O child of mine!
Time is hard,
But we will survive!
It's all in our mind!

Don't confuse your heart!
Keep it positive
(We shall overcome!)
We will reach our full potential
(We will unite!)
You and I will see the light!

I will conquer your heart!
I will gain your love
(I will reach your stars!)
I will make you love me
(I will earn your trust!)

ONE LOVE

Wrap me into your arms, babe!
And love me passionately tonight!
Look into my eyes, honey!
And get into my mind!

Reach out to my heart, darling!
And stay with me tonight!
Love me and take care of me!
Be part of this beautiful life!

No need to be alone!
No need to lose control!
None of us deserve to suffer!
I'll keep you safer!

Come and love me dearly
So we can be in control!
One love!
I'll keep you warm under the cold!

Don't feel alone!
I will love you so!
Come close to me
(O baby!)

I love you dearly!
Can you feel it!
You are everything to me!
I love you, girl, from deep in my soul!

I see you and lose control!
You are so beautiful!
This feeling is so painful!
I can't stop thinking about you!

Wrap me into your arms, babe!
And love me passionately tonight!
Look into my eyes, honey!
And get into my mind!

Reach out to my heart, darling!
And stay with me tonight!
Love me and take care of me!
Be part of this beautiful life!

No need to be alone!
No need to lose control!
None of us deserve to suffer!
I'll keep you safer!

Come and love me dearly
So we can be in control!
One love!
I'll keep you warm under the cold!

Don't feel alone!
I will love you so!
Come close to me
(O baby!)

I love you dearly!
Can you feel it!
You are everything to me!
I love you, girl, from deep in my soul!

I see you and lose control!
You are so beautiful!
This feeling is so painful!
I can't stop thinking about you!

I wanna have you
(O baby!)
I love you madly!
I'm so desperate!

I love you dearly!
Can you feel it!
You are my everything!

OPENING THE DOOR

I'm knocking on your door, baby
Can you hear me?
I'm standing in the cold, honey
Do you see me?

I love you so much, boo
Won't you come and greet me?
You set me free, little darling
For a little while!

The thought about you, sweetheart
Always makes me smile!
Won't you give me a chance to come home!
'Cause I miss you, sweetheart
And need your everlasting love!

O sweet little darling!
O sweet little thing!
To you my heart desires,
To you my soul sings!

There is a place for no sorrow
In this land of dreams!
There is a place for no pain
In this place of peace!

Don't be afraid, my lady!
Don't be afraid of me!
Don't be afraid, my darling!
Don't be afraid, my dear!

Open the door, my child!
Open the door, my queen!
Open your heart one mile!
Open the door for me!

'Cause I'm hungry and thirsty for hope!
'Cause I'm crying and begging for love!
So why don't you give me a chance to come home!
Why don't you give me a chance to rest my soul!
Why don't you give me a chance to find true love!

I will worship the Creator with all my strength!
I will worship the Almighty with all my heart!
I will sing for mercy and justice for all mankind!
I will sing for redemption in this future to come!

Please deliver the poor and the needy!
Please set them free from the rich and the greedy!
And yes, there is a place for no sorrow in this land of dreams!
There is a place for no pain in this place of peace!

Don't be afraid, my lady!
Don't be afraid of me!
Don't be afraid, my darling!
Don't be afraid, my dear!

Open the door, my child!
Open the door, my queen!
Open your heart one mile!
Open the door for me!

‘Cause I’m hungry and thirsty for hope!
‘Cause I’m crying and begging for love!
So why don’t you give me a chance to come home!
Why don’t you give me a chance to rest my soul!
Why don’t you give me a chance to find true love!

I will worship the Creator with all my strength!
I will worship the Almighty with all my heart!
I will sing for mercy and justice for all mankind!
I will sing for redemption in this future to come!

Please deliver the poor and the needy!
Please set them free from the rich and the greedy!
Open the doors to heaven and set us all free!

PLAYFUL TIME

Time to have sex!
I'm getting you wet!
Temperature is arising,
Our mind is on a trance!

I'm holding your hips!
I'm pulling your hair!
I'm biting your lips!
I'm licking your breast!

I'm making you scream!
I'm making you reach your climax
Again and again!

There's no time to waste!
Let's do it again!
Let's make our love last forever
With no regrets!

Te amo de verdad!
No resistas mas!
Agamos el amor!
Siempre juntos asta la muerte!

Flor de piel!
Mi regalo del Edén!
Sonrisa inolvidable!
Labios de miel!

Let's do it again!
On the couch, on the floor!
On the bathroom, on our bed!
In the car and everywhere!

Let this passion carry us away!
Let this playful moment lead our way!
Let our soul be blazed!
Let our body rest!

Let us travel in a trance!
Let us do this all over again!
Let's enjoy the night!
This is our playful time!

Let's make love under the sun!
Under the moon and the stars!
Let us love each other
In the time we meet!

Let us love each other, honey, and be freed!
Let us remain together, babe,
Because together, honey—
Together is what we're supposed to be!

Te amo de verdad!
No resistas mas!
Agamos el amor!
Siempre juntos asta la muerte!

Flor de piel!
Mi regalo del Edén!
Sonrisa inolvidable!
Labios de miel!

Let's do it again!
On the couch, on the floor!
On the bathroom, on our bed!
In the car and everywhere!

Let this passion carry us away!
Let this playful moment lead our way!
Let our soul be blazed!
Let our body rest!

Let us travel in a trance!
Let us do this all over again!
Let's enjoy the night!
This is our playful time!

Let's make love under the sun!
Under the moon and the stars!
Let us love each other, darling,
In the time we meet!

Let us love each other, honey, and be freed!
Let us remain together, babe,
Because together, honey—
Together is what we're supposed to be!

REMINISCING THE ACT OF PLEASURE

On the first night of our first date!
I touched the stars of her deep brown face
(In a unique and beautiful warm day)
Of great passion and sweet loving pain!

I have felt her wet and warm body within my bare hands!
And have smelled her personal and unique essence!
I have woken up the desires inside her flesh!
And have explored the nakedness between her legs!

I have sinned in the flesh on that day!
In a pure love of sweet desires in that motel!
My eyes were too busy contemplating her beautiful face!
Now I cannot forget making love until the next bright day!

We both wanted to escalate
From being friends to becoming lovers right away!

My body all over her body dancing with no regrets!
My thoughts and her thoughts were united in this loving game!
My hands and her hands were touching and caressing ourselves!

I was able to kiss her all over her neck!
I was able to lick her all over her breast!
I made her scream my name on that bed!
I made her mine again and again!

Now I just reminisce that beautiful act of pleasure on that hotel's
bed
I wish I can see her again!
But she is too many miles away!

I wish I can caress again her nakedness within my own bare hands!
I wish I can lick her all over her breast!
Now I just reminisce that beautiful act of pleasure that happened
on that day!

SEXING YOU AND SQUEEZING YOU

I'm gonna kiss you softly, babe
Squeeze you roughly
Put my arms around you gently
Sex you passionately

Your whole face is so lovely
Your body is so exotic
I'm gonna love you so emotional
Your loving is so magical

I cannot wait to make you mine
Give you all my life
Making love in this passionate night
You're so unforgettable, so incredible

I cannot stop loving you
Touching you
Kissing you
Playing with you
Putting my arms all around you
Sexing you

Can you just be loving me?
By staying with me
Giving me all this sexual medicine
Carrying me
Holding me

Your lips are so sweet
Baby, you are my queen
And I am your king
Sexually living the ecstasy

Jumping all over me
Squeezing me
Kissing me
Loving me
Taking good care of me

Humbly. Honestly
By being with me
In this reality
Fantasy
You make me lose my mind

I think about you at all times
You are the perfect love
I wanna know if you're coming for sure
So I can wait for you

My love is for you
Day by day
Night by night

I wanna hold you tight
Keep you in my arms
Kissing your sweet mouth
Reaching for the stars while looking into your eyes

You're in my heart
You're all I want
Please stay with me in this sweet life

Holding me
Loving me
Sexing me
Taking good care of me

In this reality
Fantasy
Magically
Ecstasy

Don't stop loving me
And keep on loving me
As I love you
'Cause you're my boo

This poetry is all for you
I know for sure that my love is you

In this awesome mood
We will always bloom
Me and you loving each other in our honeymoon

Loving each other
Holding each other
Sexing each other
Fantastically. Magically. Spontaneously

Until the end of the times
Our love will rise
In these romantic nights
You and I throughout the stages of life

SHE'S MY NUMBER ONE

She's only mine
And she's the only one
She makes me feel so fine
And there's no other one

I have her in mind, bro
So close to my heart
Loving her day and night

I don't want to make her cry
I have to make her laugh
Holding her and squeezing her real tight

She's the best in this life, bro
She's the roots of my heart
The sight to my eyes
The thoughts in my mind

She's my number one
She's the love of my life
She's the one that I want

I wish I could hold her tight
Caress her body all night
Give her a kiss good night
Can't take her out of my mind

In these hard times
Don't wanna say goodbye
She's the best thing in my life
She's my number one
She's the one I want

Love is the key of all needs and wants
Unification is our purpose of life
Happiness is all we want
Satisfaction is keeping us alive

Come and be part of this awesome life
Come and be happy tonight
Come and I'll keep you warm

Let's just waste no time
You're the one I want
You're the number one

Look into my eyes, baby
Let's make love tonight
Let's enter into paradise
Let's love each other all night
Let's forget the present and past

Tonight is our loving night
I'll give you my love
I'll give you my life

I'll give you all the affection
I'll give you all my time
I'll be gentle and kind
I'll be captain of this mystical ride

We'll be all right
We'll be just fine
We'll be loving each other for the rest of our lives

I will be your number one
I will be the man that you desire and want
I'll be together with you for the rest of my life

So don't treat me bad
Love me with all your heart
'Cause I'll be together with you for the rest of this life

SING TO ME, BABE

The weather is so beautiful today!
The sky is so clear with a beautiful sunset!
And I'm happy like a hummingbird!
I'm so content!

I'm so blessed every single day!
Because I'm coming closer to you!
Because I want to kiss you, honey!
I want to kiss you in a very special way!

I love it when you sing to me!
I love it, babe
(Oh yes, in thee!)
I feel so happy like the plants and the trees!

I feel so happy like the ocean breeze!
I feel so happy like the seven seas!
I feel so happy like the heavens above and the earth beneath!

Oh, I love it when you sing to me!
I love it, babe
(Oh yes, in thee!)

Life is meant to be enjoyed and feel free!
Life is meant to feel happy living in peace!

So come to me, babe!
Come to me, darling, and set me free!
Because your mind is in denial!
And because your sweet love belongs to me!

I'm here to feel loved!
I'm here to feel freed!
I'm here to kiss you softly!
I'm here to set myself free!

So come to me, little woman, and stay with me!
Oh, I love it when you sing to me, honey!
I love it, babe
(Oh yes, in thee!)

Life is meant to be enjoyed and feel free!
Life is meant to feel happy living in peace!

So come to me, babe!
Come to me, darling, and set me free!
Because your mind is in denial!
And because your sweet love belongs to me!

I'm here to feel loved!
I'm here to feel freed!
I'm here to kiss you softly!
I'm here to set myself free!

So come to me, little woman,
And stay with me!
Stay for the rest of your life
Together forever with me

SING TO ME, BABE, AND ROCK THE MIC

I saw my girl singing to me last night (O God!)
She was shining so bright like a rock star!

Sing to me, baby, and rock the mic!
Look into my eyes, baby, and reach my heart!
Sing to me, baby, and rock the mic!
Forget about the world and hold me tight!

Sing to me, baby, and rock the mic!
Let the spirit touch you, honey, you'll be fine!
Sing to me, baby, and rock the mic!
Don't let anyone stop you 'cause I'm loving you tonight!

Sing to me, baby, and rock the mic!
Love me, darling, as I'm loving you in this awesome night!
Sing to me, baby, and rock the mic!
Drift away in a trance, and enjoy of my loving night after night!

Sing to me, baby, and rock the mic!
Love me, babe, so passionately until the morning comes!
Sing to me, baby, and rock the mic!
Stay with me tonight, and remain playfully throughout the stages
of life!

Sing to me, baby, and rock the mic!
Promise me, honey, you will love me forever as I love you with all
my heart!
Sing to me, baby, and rock the mic!
Make love to me, darling, under the moon and the stars!

Sing to me, baby, and rock the mic!
Have dinner with me with flowers and some candle lights!
Sing to me, baby, and rock the mic!
Dance with me tonight and hold me, babe, so firm and so tight!

Sing to me, baby, and rock the mic!
Let the music be our guide, and love me, honey, like no one in this
life!
Sing to me, baby, and rock the mic!
Feel the love, darling, and be satisfied!

Sing to me, baby, and rock the mic!
Don't stop loving me, babe,
And I won't stop loving you, honey,
Until our final day's arrived!

SPEND SOME TIME WITH ME

Come out to the fields, little woman, to hear me sing!
Come out from wherever you are, sweet little thing!

Don't let anyone ruin your dreams!
Don't let your eyes melt into tears!
Don't let your emotions get you sick!
Don't let your decisions get you away from me!

'Cause tonight, sweet little thing,
You will be happy spending some time with me!

Nobody is able to feel these emotions that I'm feeling inside of me!
Nobody is able to feel the necessity of having you next to me!
So let this music satisfy your internal needs!
Let this love get you closer and closer to me!

'Cause tonight, sweet little thing,
You will be happy and satisfied with me!

I have seen the most beautiful thing!
I have desired your sweet company!
I have created this mellow beat!
I have decided to bring you closer and closer to me!

'Cause tonight, sweet little thing,
You will be happy and satisfied with me!

So come out to the fields, little woman, to hear me sing!
Come out from wherever you are, sweet little thing!

Don't let anyone ruin your dreams!
Don't let your eyes melt into tears!
Don't let your emotions get you sick!
Don't let your decisions get you away from me!

'Cause tonight, sweet little thing,
You will be happy spending some time with me!

SPIRITUAL HEALING TIME

Beauty comes from within ourselves!
Beauty comes from within our inner self!
True happiness comes by itself!
True happiness comes from ourselves!

So don't feel forsaken, sweet child!
Don't feel left out in this bitterness!
Because my door is open for you, babe!
Because my heart is open for you, honey!
Because my soul is ready to love you, darling, in this beautiful life!

Time is going to heal any pain in your heart, honey!
Time is going to allow you to leave everything behind, babe!
So let's unite and get together tonight!
Let's get together and love each other in life!

Because the mood is so sweet!
Because the time is so fine!
Because my heart and soul are willing
(Are willing, darling)
Are willing to hold you tight!

In this time of unification, honey!
In this time of redemption, darling!
In this time of consolation, babe!
In this beautiful time!

The mood is so sweet!
The time is so fine!
My soul is willing, babe
(It's willing, darling)
It's willing to hold you tight!

Because the mood is so sweet!
Because the time is so fine!
Because my heart and soul are willing
(Are willing, darling)
Are willing to hold you tight!

In this time of unification, honey!
In this time of redemption, darling!
In this time of consolation, babe!
In this beautiful time!

The mood is so sweet!
The time is so fine!
My soul is willing, babe
(It's willing, darling)
It's willing to hold you tight!

THE POWER OF LOVE

I could picture your body next to me, babe!
The sensation of your lips getting next to me!
The persuasion of these feelings
That enable me to experience your unique and everlasting ecstasy!

I do need your loving to quench this thirst!
Girl, would you please be my nurse;
Lift me up and heal me when I am disturbed!
I do want your company to release this negativity in me!

I do need of your presence to set me free from all this grief!
Because without you, honey, nothing else matters to me!
Because with you, darling, my whole life is complete!
I do need your loving next to me!

Because to me, girl, you are my everything!
I feel deprived of happiness when I am away from you!
Because with you, boo, my life is not just shiny and blue!
It is realistic and humanistic when it's part of you!

I wanna hold you tight and never let you go!
Because you were sent from heaven above to give me love!
I don't feel alone anymore when the days are cold!
Because all the sad moments are replaced with happiness and joy!

I want to smile when the times are tough!
Because I love you, girl, more than you've ever known!
So here I go again alone in these raining days!
Feeling pain inside my chest!
Hoping to see you sooner one of these days!

Here I go speaking out rhymes from deep in my soul!
Here I go loving you madly, babe!
Needing you badly under the rain and the cold!

We hear the rumors and sounds of Third World War!
But it is just the big corporations trying to establish power and
control!
They manipulate the media and religion all along!
They want to terrorize us and separate us even more!

We love each other more than money and gold!
We believe in resistance and the power of love!
I don't feel alone anymore when the days are cold!
Because all the sad moments are replaced with happiness and joy!

I want to smile when the times are tough!
Because I love you, girl, more than you've ever known!
So here I go again alone in these raining days!
Feeling pain inside my chest!
Hoping to see you sooner one of these days!

Here I go speaking out rhymes from deep in my soul!
Here I go loving you madly, babe!
Needing you badly under the rain and the cold!

We hear the rumors and sounds of Third World War!
But it is just the big corporations trying to establish power and
control!
They manipulate the media and religion all along!
They want to terrorize us and separate us even more!

We love each other more than money and gold!
We believe in resistance and the power of love!

THE THINGS OF LOVE

There's no right or wrong in the things of love
There's no more or less to reach success
It takes two to make it work
It takes two to play the game

I could be right,
But it could be wrong
Whatever we decide,
It will make us love us more

With you, there's no stress
Without you, I get depressed
My love for you will always be strong
In the things of love, you are the boss

We shall love and hate
We shall serve and reign
We shall love each other
We shall be together every moment that we can

You are the peacefulness I seek
You are the happiness in me
You are the phrases of this poetry
You are my destiny

You are my life
You are my baby
You are what my heart needs and wants

I haven't felt this way before
It seems like love has opened this special door
I will intend to love you
I will intend to adore you
I will intend to take care of you every moment that I can

I see your face, and my heart cannot sustain
The thought of loving you, baby, every single day
So I pray to the heavens above to let me stay
I see in your face sweetness loving me again and again

With you, honey, I accomplish any struggle, boo
Without you, I'm lost and confused

I'm falling for you
I'm crazy about you
I'm loving you, babe, caring for you
Making love to you

In my dreams thinking of you
And in this life dying for you
Crazy for love
Drinking alone
Missing you, darling, for this long

THINKING ABOUT YOU AND WANTING YOU

The sky is so blue, baby
The ocean is so cool
My mind is thinking of you
My heart is loving you

You're so close to my heart
You're so close to my soul
You're so close to my eyes
You're so close to my love

I'm loving you, darling
I'm missing you
I'm wanting you, honey
I'm desiring you

Hours passed, and I'm still thinking about you
Minutes had passed, and I'm still loving you
The day goes on, and I'm wanting you
The evening comes, and I'm still desiring you

The night also comes, and I'm still seeing you
You're on my mind every single day and night
You're in my heart, baby
Running up and down all the time

And I can't deny, darling,
I love you
I love the way you are

Could this be love?
Could it be a fantasy?
Could I be lost?
Could I be dreaming?

I'm loving you, honey
And that's the way I'm living it

Thinking about you
Loving you
Wishing to be with you
Desiring you
All day long

I can't move on
I need to have you
You can't be gone
I need you in my life
I need you all the time

Your love is all I want
If I don't have you, I prefer to rather die
You are my light on this darkened path
You're my guide
Wherever I'm at

I need you in my life
I need you day and night
If I don't have you, baby,
I prefer, my sweet love, to rather die

Life would be meaningless without you by my side
Time would be timeless without you in my heart
You have to stay with me, honey
No matter what

In the good times
And the bad times
You have to stick with me, darling
Now and in the future to come

TRAVELING THROUGH YOUR WHOLE BEING

I found myself in the woods, babe!
O how sweet it is to be thinking of you!
I found myself in a trance, honey!
O how beautiful it is to be trapped in your nest!

You make me feel like a flying bird!
You make me feel like a downstream river on a curve!

I run slowly sometimes
(O yes, I do, honey!)
I run shifting velocities through your mind!

It gets me flying through the sky!
It gets me traveling into your mind!
It gets me flowing into your soul!
It gets me resting into your heart!

Que bonito, que bonito, babe, que bonito!
It is to travel through your whole being, pasito a pasito!
Que sabroso, que sabroso, honey, que sabroso!
It is to taste your beautiful lips, con mucho amor y con mucho gozo!

※ ※ ※

'Cause you make me feel like a flying bird!
'Cause you make me feel like a downstream river on a curve!
'Cause I am able to run slowly sometimes!
'Cause I am able to shift velocities through your mind!

Que bonito, que bonito, babe, que bonito!
Que sabroso, que sabroso, honey, que sabroso!

It gets me flying through the sky!
It gets me traveling into your mind!
It gets me flowing into your soul!
It gets me resting into your heart!

Que bonito, que bonito, babe, que bonito!
Que sabroso, que sabroso, honey, que sabroso!

It gets me flying through the sky!
It gets me traveling into your mind!
It gets me flowing into your soul!
It gets me resting into your heart!

Que bonito, que bonito, babe, que bonito!
It is to travel through your whole being, pasito a pasito!
Que sabroso, que sabroso, honey, que sabroso!
It is to taste your beautiful lips, con mucho amor y con mucho
gozo!

'Cause you make me feel like a flying bird!
'Cause you make me feel like a downstream river on a curve!
'Cause I am able to run slowly sometimes!
'Cause I am able to shift velocities through your mind!

Que bonito, que bonito, babe, que bonito!
Que sabroso, que sabroso, honey, que sabroso!

It gets me flying through the sky!
It gets me traveling into your mind!
It gets me flowing into your soul!
It gets me resting into your heart!

Que bonito, que bonito, babe, que bonito!
Que sabroso, que sabroso, honey, que sabroso!

It gets me flying through the sky!
It gets me traveling into your mind!
It gets me flowing into your soul!
It gets me resting into your heart!

Que bonito, que bonito, babe, que bonito!
It is to travel through your whole being, pasito a pasito!
Que sabroso, que sabroso, honey, que sabroso!
It is to taste your beautiful lips, con mucho amor y con mucho
gozo!

TURNING LOOSE

Where is the moon?
Where is the sun?
Where is my happiness tonight?

I know I should be moving forward
Like a flying bird in the sky!
I know I should be flying away from the past
And leaving everything behind!

But here I am again
Meditating alone in the dark!
Here I am praying to the Most High!
Praying for both of us alone in this lonely night!

'Cause only you
Can bring satisfaction in my heart!
'Cause only you
Can understand the tribulations held in my mind!

And here I am alone in the dark!
Here I am hoping to see you tonight!
Here I am reciting new psalms to the Most High!

Tears are falling down my eyes!
Tears are falling down my eyes, babe!
'Cause I miss you so much (I miss you, babe!)
I've been missing you all this time!

Here I am wrongly accused
(Here I am, babe!)
Here I am feeling so blue!

But through the powers of the Most High!
I will find the way to turn myself loose!

I wish I can be happy next to you!
I wish I can stay for a longer time, boo!
I wish you could understand that I am trying so hard too!

But I've been tied down, boo!
I've been trapped in captivity,
And I'm trying to turn myself loose!

I am a rebel, babe, what can I say!
I am a man who travels from place to place!
Don't let my culture stress you today!
Don't let my words scare you away!

'Cause I am wrongly accused!
'Cause I am wrongly abused!
'Cause I am wrongly tied down, boo!

But through the powers of the Most High,
I will find the way to turn myself loose!

WALK NEXT TO ME

The love I feel for you
Is as simple as the light of the sun and the air we breathe
As important as the food that nourishes our being
And the dream that makes me live the moment I met you

You brought happiness and set me free from loneliness and grief!
Your love is like a beautiful flower!
You are that flower from this special garden!
You lift me up when I am in need!
You give me company and always take good care of me!

Your smile is so intense, babe!
Your lips are so unique!
Your tenderness is so great, honey!
Your kisses are so sweet!

The moment is so great!
The experience is so perfect!
The time is so lasting when you are next to me!

I'm not looking for money or digging for gold, honey!
All I need is your sweet love, babe!
Kiss you softly with unconditional love!

Let this love lead the way!
Let these feelings stay!
Let my love for you forever be there!
Let us remain together and be blessed!
Let us join each other's company and live together among this
earth!

Hold my hand and walk next to me in this road of life!
Be there for me, and I'll be there for you, sweet child of mine!
Dry your eyes and smile through the stages of life!
Be there to lift me up, and I'll be here to love you and protect you
with my own life!

Because your love is like a beautiful flower, girl!
And you are that flower from this special garden!
You lift me up when I am in need!
You give me company and always take good care of me!

Your smile is so intense, babe!
Your lips are so unique!
Your tenderness is so great, honey!
Your kisses are so sweet!

The moment is so great!
The experience is so perfect!
The time is so lasting when you are next to me!

I'm not looking for money or digging for gold, honey!
All I need is your sweet love, babe!
Kiss you softly with unconditional love!

Let this love lead the way!
Let these feelings stay!
Let my love for you forever be there!
Let us remain together and be blessed!
Let us join each other's company and live together upon this earth!

Hold my hand and walk next to me in this road of life!
Be there for me, and I'll be there for you, sweet child of mine!
Dry your eyes and smile through the stages of life!
Be there to lift me up, and I'll be here to love you and protect you
with my own life!

YOU ARE MY POETRY

Hello, my sweet love
Just want you to know
That I'm keeping control
Of all the emotions
Held in my soul

You are so gentle and so sweet
You are so kind and so genuine
Your beauty is so extreme
Your tenderness is so supreme
You are so spectacular for my eyes to see
You are so impressive and full of good energy

I will never find
A woman so magnificent and so fine
In this lifetime

I see you and I making love in this passionate night
You're on my mind and in my heart
I see the moon, the sun, and the starts
When I kiss your sweet mouth

You lift me up when hard times come
In my tribulations, you restore my heart
You wipe the tears from my eyes from time to time
And in the sad days, you comfort my mind

Your kisses are so sweet
So special and so unique
Your voice is like a melody
So lovely and so inspiring

You're like a honeybee
A queen like it's supposed to be
Taking good care of me
In this destiny

You're always in my dreams
Making me believe that you're everything
And in this reality,
You are this poetry

You are the poetry of a love song
The rhythm of a drum
The effects of tobacco and rum
The desires of making love

With you, I can reach the sky
You take me into paradise
You make me feel so alive
Your sweet love is mine

You'll always be right
You fulfill my entire life
You're the light of the sun
You're the sound of the mic

When you speak,
Everything is so calm
You are the star in the sky
You are this poetry and the rhymes

You are my babe and my future wife
You are the sight of my eyes
The colors of the rainbow in the sky
You are just the poetry of these meaningful lines

YOU NEVER KNOW WHAT YOU GOT UNTIL IT'S GONE

Thinking about past memories!
Loving people like my own family!
We can only laugh! We can only cry!
We can only bullshit and live life!

You never know what you got until it's gone!
We think back!
We feel sad!
We laugh and move on!

I could walk upon the hills at night!
I could raise your desires tonight!
I could burn your desires and fire, babe!
I could make love to you and make you reach the stars!

You are so beautiful
Like the rising sun!
You are so special, honey,
Like the moon and the stars!

Your lips were taken from a sugarcane!
Your eyes were made from a diamond blend!
Your body was created so desirable, darling,
For the envy of many men!

I see you in my dreams, girl,
Every time I go to bed!
I close my eyes and contemplate
Your beautiful and lovely face!

I love you and miss you every single day!
I think I'm losing my head!
The memories about you
Are really hard to erase!

My love for you is really easy to explain!
I need you in my life, babe, more than water and air!
I need you in my life, honey,
Because without you, my whole life is meaningless!

Things we cannot change!
Things we cannot complain!
Things we can only embrace and live on!

You used to smell so nice!
Your mouth used to taste like cherry pie!
You used to be so sweet!
Your smile, honey, was so special to me!

Your voice used to sound like a sweet melody!
And your company, darling
Your company is all I need!

I see you in my dreams, girl,
Every time I go to bed!
I close my eyes and contemplate
Your beautiful and lovely face!

I love you and miss you every single day!
I think I'm losing my head!
The memories about you
Are really hard to erase!

My love for you is really easy to explain!
I need you in my life, babe, more than water and air!
I need you in my life, honey,
Because without you, my whole life is meaningless!

Things we cannot change!
Things we cannot complain!
Things we can only embrace and live on!

You used to smell so nice!
Your mouth used to taste like cherry pie!
You used to be so sweet!
Your smile, honey, was so special to me!

Your voice used to sound like a sweet melody!
And your company, darling
Your company is all I need!

YOU SET ME FREE

You came to me, babe, like the sunlight on the sky!
You cleared all the tears on my eyes!
You brought the light to the darkest side of my life!
You brought happiness and love to my heart!
You set my mind free from pain and political lies!

The water from the ocean is so fresh, babe!
Your lips are so sweet!
Your smile is so intense!
Your breath is so unique!

The moment is so perfect!
The time is so lasting when you are next to me!

My heart is dying, babe!
My soul is crying!
My wishes and desires to see you are greater than this beautiful
sun!

You give me shelter when the night arrives!
You give me company when the shadows come!
You give me loving, sweet little babe!
You give me loving when the moon has gone from my side!

Tu cuerpo está lleno de poesía, mi nena!
Tu voz mamita chula está llena de alegría!
Tu aliento es perfume a mi vida!
Tu sombra me acompaña día tras día!

U qué bonito se siente cuando estoy contigo!
U qué bien se siente cuando estás conmigo!

Las luces de los cielos, Mami, se neutralizan!
Las aguas de los mares, Bebe, se tranquilizan!
Las fuerzas de los vientos, Nena, se normalizan!
Las pupilas de mis ojos, Chiquilla, se regocijan!

U qué bonito se siente cuando estoy contigo!
U qué bien se siente cuando estás conmigo!
Todo se ve muy bien, Mamita, en este anochecer!
Todo se ve muy bien, Nenita, en este amanecer!

Las luces de los cielos, Mami, se neutralizan!
Las aguas de los mares, Bebe, se tranquilizan!
Las fuerzas de los vientos, Nena, se normalizan!
Las pupilas de mis ojos, Chiquilla, se regocijan!

My heart is dying, babe!
My soul is crying!
My wishes and desires to see you
Are greater than this beautiful sun!

You give me shelter when the night arrives!
You give me company when the shadows come!
You give me your loving, sweet little babe!
You give me your loving when the moon has gone from my side!

POESÍA

ALMA JUSTICIERA

El amor que le tengo a la justicia
Es muy simple de explicar
En un conjunto de palabras
Libres como el viento y el mar
Es un sentimiento muy bello
Que solo el alma lo sabe apreciar
Es la esperanza de todo ser humano
Y el deseo de vivir en libertad

La vida sigue—Sigue la vida
A través del tiempo sin parar
La lucha sigue—Sigue la lucha
Más fuerte que un huracán
El amor verdadero se siente,
Se siente por las venas al pasar
El orgullo y sentimiento del pueblo
Se demuestra al vivir en igualdad

El alma de un ser humano
No se vende como azúcar y pan
La sobrevivencia de un infante
No se le niega nunca—Jamas
Por eso yo soy libre al pensar
Por eso yo soy libre al amar
Por eso yo te canto, Alma Justiciera,
Con orgullo y dignidad.

Mi alma se llena de gozo
Al sonido del tambor
Las nuves se llenan de puesia
A través de mi imaginación
Yo te saludo, mi linda flor,
Yo te recibo en mi corazón
Yo te nombro Alma Justiciera
Simbolo de pureza y amor

AMANDONOS EN ESTE INMENSO EDEN

Soy libre como el viento
Soy libre como el agua del Mar
Soy libre para llenarte de besos
Soy libre para poderte amar

Te amo eternamente
Te amo por tu dulce mirar
Te amo francamente
Te amo desde la orilla del Mar

Tu eres la mujer de mi vida
Tu eres la mujer ideal
Tu eres la más consentida
Tu eres una mujer muy genial

Mi Flor de piel
Mi florecita del Edén
Mi dulce Amor
Mi hermosura de mujer
Mi lindo amanecer
Mi pintoresco atardecer

Me seduces con tu dulce amor
Me cautivas con tu sincero querer
Vamos amarnos bajo nuestro techo
Vamos a unir mi piel con tu piel

Bajo la luz de la Luna
Bajo la luz de el Sol
Bajo miles de estrellas
Bajo el paraíso de este inmenso Edén
Quisiera poder

Quisiera tener tus dulce labios con sabor a miel
Disfrutar del momento y perderme en tu ser
Gozando del Amor
Juntos tu y yo

Un suspiro excitante con mucho amor y placer
Mi cuerpo y tu cuerpo se dan a entender
Ensendiendo la llama excitante de nuestra caliente piel
Sintiendo el amor por primera vez

Amandonos locamente ardiendo en placer
Mi piel con tu piel, mi princesa hermosa, amandonos en este
inmenso Edén.

AVENTURA DE AMOR

El destino
Mi Niña
Te puso en mi camino
Mujer cara de ángel
Sonrisa inolvidable
Sencillez
Ojos de miel mirada espeluznante cuerpo divino

Yo suspiro
MaMi
En el fondo de mi alma
El placer de acariciarte
Entre mis manos abrazarte
Porque admiro tu belleza
Desde el primer momento
En que a mi vida llegaste!

Como una flor
Te Miro Yo
En mi corazón
Esta canción
Te canto yo, para que sepas—
Muy seriamente
MaMi
El sentimiento que dejaste!

En un rio de pasion
Es mi ilusion
Besar tus labios,
Acariciar tu pelo,
Viajar muy lentamente
Entre la sima de tus senos!

Como un vaso de vino
Tomarte entre mis labios
Acariciarte lentamente
Beber de tus caricias,
Embriagarme de pasion
Con el sabor—y el perfume de tus besos

Entre la luna y el sol
Hacerte el amor!
Llenarte de placer
De la noche al amanecer!
A través de la distancia y el tiempo
Llenarnos de pasión
Hacer una Aventura de Amor
Llevando nuestros cuerpos hasta la cumbre mas oculta del cielo

QUIEN TE AMARA COMO LO HACIA YO

Quien te ara el amor
con loca pasión
como lo hacia yo
por las lindas mañanas

Recordarte que eres mía
navegando por tu cuerpo
en la oscuridad de la noche
y en la luz del día

Llenándote de besos
por todas partes de tu ser
y acariciandote tus pechos

Bajándote un montón de estrellas
poniendolas en tus manos
para apreciar la luz de ellas

Mojando tus partes íntimas
e intercambiando caricias
y gestos al amarte

Complaciendo todas tus fantasías
y tus más profundos deseos
Caminando de la mano
y disiendote al oído lo mucho que te quiero

Para asi poder amarnos mutuamente
A través de la distancia y el tiempo
Uniendo nuestras almas y nuestros cuerpos.
Formando un hogar lleno de amor y dulce sentimientos

PEACE

AGAPE LOVE

Nobody is with me today!
Nobody is with me, it's okay!
Nobody is with me
In this lonely day (nobody!)

I feel scared, like a newborn child
(Oh yes, babe!)
I feel hurt like a good soldier in battle
(Oh yes, honey!)
I feel lost like a sheep in the wild, but it's okay!

I am a man with deep emotions!
I am a train with locomotion!
I am a tree planted with lots of strength
(Oh yes, babe!)

Only the Creator knows my secrets
(Oh yes, Lord!)
Only Yahweh knows my tribulations
(Oh yes, Lord!)
Only God will carry me to Zion when I'm gone!

Many people pretend they love me now
(They do!)
Many people come to me and smile
(Yes, they do!)
Many people are selfish
And don't understand what love can bring!

But I am happy like the sun and the rain!
I am happy every single day!

Because no selfish man
Can take away the peace in my soul
(No one can!)
Because no evil woman
Can take away the happiness in my heart
(No one can!)

Because none of my enemies
Can take away my freedom within!
Because my inner strength
Comes from agape love!

FINDING REDEMPTION (SPIRITUAL WAR)

There comes their master dressed in new clothes!
There comes his new system to enslave us even more!
There comes his lady to join the party for sure!
There comes the great beast riding his lady around the world!

He will try to defeat me,
For I'm telling the truth!
He will try to confuse me,
For I know his final doom!

But I will not be afraid!
I will not be confused!
I will remain standing strong
In this Armageddon for sure!

We are the indigenous people claiming for rights!
We are the Mesoamericans uprising in our own land!
We don't want our children to live in oppression!
We don't want their dreams to die in transgression!

Because we have been taken for granted for so long!
Because the dominant culture has been suppressing this truth in
their history and their laws!
Because rich people have been taking advantage of poor people all
along
Because we are coming strong
Because we are coming from the cold

O Rabbi, El Shaddai, Adonai, Elohim!
Clean my mind, my heart, and my spirit!
Let me reach Mount Zion and rest in peace!

For my mind is thirsty for understanding!
For my heart is hungry for love!

Let me free myself and be emancipated in body and soul!
Let me reach full equality here on earth so I can finally grow

LIVING WATER

Sweet living water
(Sweet living water)
Sweet living water from a living spring!

O sweet living soul
(Sweet living soul)
Sweet living soul of a human being!

How confused you have lived!
How corrupt
(How corrupt)
How corrupt you have been!

Lift up your eyes to heaven
(Lift up your eyes to heaven)
Lift up your eyes to heaven and remember (remember)
Remember your old deeds!

People will try to eliminate me
With new philosophies and political laws!
People will try to segregate me
With new strategies coming from their loss!

But I am a free man like the clouds and the flying birds!
I am as free as any other man!
And until you treat me like any ordinary man!
I won't listen to whatever you got to say!

O sweet living water
(Sweet living water)
Sweet living water from a living spring!

O sweet living soul
(Sweet living soul)
Sweet living soul of a human being!

How confused you have lived!
How corrupt
(How corrupt)
How corrupt you have been!

Lift up your eyes to heaven
(Lift up your eyes to heaven)
Lift up your eyes to heaven and remember (remember)
Remember your old deeds!

People will try to eliminate me
With new philosophies and political laws!
People will try to segregate me
With new strategies coming from their loss!

But I am a free man like the clouds and the flying birds!
I am as free as any other man!
And until you treat me like any ordinary man!
I won't listen to whatever you got to say!

NEW PSALM: "REBELUTIONARY"

I'm so happy, so happy, so happy tonight!
I'm so glad, so glad, so glad to be alive!
I'm so grateful, so grateful, so grateful inside!
I'm so thankful, so thankful, so thankful to the Most High!

Mi canto es como una flor!
Mi gozo es como una rosa!
Mi canto es como una expresión de una manera muy hermosa!

And I'm so happy, so happy, so happy tonight!
I'm so glad, so glad, so glad to be alive!
I'm so grateful, so grateful, so grateful inside!
I'm so thankful, so thankful, so thankful to the Most High!

I will worship the Almighty with all my strength!
I will worship the Creator with all my heart!
I will sing songs of freedom and redemption to the Most High!
I will sing for mercy and justice for all mankind!

Oh, hear the cry, the cry, the cry of this humble heart!
Oh, hear the plea, the plea, the plea of many of us!
Oh, hear the songs, the songs, the songs coming from our heart!
Hear the psalms, the psalms, the psalms from the oppressed ones!

Because we are crying, we are crying, we are crying aloud!
Because we are weeping, we are weeping, we are weeping tonight!
Because we are lost in captivity in our own land!
Because we are pleading for mercy and acceptance in these hard
times!

You have planted this beautiful song in my heart!
You have given this beautiful psalm to all mankind!
You have given us your blessings to the humble ones!

I'm so happy, so happy, so happy tonight!
I'm so glad, so glad, so glad to be alive!
I'm so grateful, so grateful, so grateful inside!
I'm so thankful, so thankful, so thankful to the Most High!

Mi canto es como una flor!
Mi gozo es como una rosa!
Mi canto es como una expresión de una manera muy hermosa!

And I'm so happy, so happy, so happy tonight!
I'm so glad, so glad, so glad to be alive!
I'm so grateful, so grateful, so grateful inside!
I'm so thankful, so thankful, so thankful to the Most High!

I will worship the Almighty with all my strength!
I will worship the Creator with all my heart!
I will sing songs of freedom and redemption to the Most High!
I will sing for mercy and justice for all mankind!

Oh, hear the cry, the cry, the cry of my humble heart!
Oh, hear the plea, the plea, the plea of many of us!
Oh, hear the songs, the songs, the songs coming from our heart!
Hear the psalms, the psalms, the psalms from the oppressed ones!

Because we are crying, we are crying, we are crying aloud!
Because we are weeping, we are weeping, we are weeping tonight!
Because we are lost in captivity in our own land!
Because we are pleading for mercy and acceptance in these hard
times!

You have planted this beautiful song in my heart!
You have given this beautiful psalm to all mankind!
You have given us your blessings to the humble ones!

THE SPIRITUAL ROOTS

At the end,
Love will overcome everything!
At the end,
The golden city will shine completely!

There shall be no more night!
There shall be no more crying!
There shall be no more death!
There shall be no more sorrow!
There shall be no more pain!

For corruption and hypocrisy
Will pass away!
For King Alpha and Father Omega
Will carry us away!

Because they are the Light!
Because they are the Fire!
The Living Fire
That burns down everything!

Lots of people believe
That they are the Living Tree!
Lots of people claim
That they are the chosen ones the Almighty has conceived!

So if they are the Living Tree,
Then I am the roots (the living roots) planted beneath!
And without the foundation,
The Living Tree will fall down to the firepit!

The roots want to grow into branches!
The roots want to grow into big trees!
So let the roots give life to the Living Tree!
Let them both live forever in Mount Zion in harmony and peace!